# SLAYING SARASOTA

Curated by Leigh M. Clark

Aurora Corialis Publishing

Pittsburgh, PA

# Table of Contents

# Introduction: Sarasota, Stories, and the Strength of Women

## Leigh M. Clark

Sarasota is one of those rare places that surprises you. At first glance, it's postcard-perfect—white sand beaches, turquoise waters, sunsets so beautiful they make you believe in something bigger. But spend some time here, and you'll see there's so much more beneath the surface. This is a city where history and progress coexist, where creativity thrives alongside industry, and where resilience isn't just a word—it's a way of life.

People come to Sarasota for different reasons. Some arrive looking for a fresh start, some for the inspiration that comes from being surrounded by art and culture, and some for the sense of community that makes this place feel like home. But no matter how they get here, one thing is certain: the women of Sarasota don't just live here—they shape it.

They are leaders, innovators, and trailblazers. They build businesses, create art, raise families, and advocate for change. And yet, so often, we only see the surface of their lives—the job titles, the social media posts, the highlight reels.

I launched Slay the USA because I wanted to go deeper.

### The Why Behind This Movement

I started this movement to share who the women in each city truly are—not just what they do, but the journeys that shaped them. The obstacles they've faced. The moments that changed everything. Because how often do we really get to know someone's story? Not just the version they share at networking events, but the real, raw truth of what it took to get here?

Our stories matter. They connect us, they teach us, they remind us that we're not alone. They are our legacy. And when we have the courage to share them—not just the polished parts, but the struggles and triumphs in between—we give others permission to do the same.

That's what Slay the USA is about. It's a national series dedicated to showcasing the untold stories of women who are shaping their cities—women who are building businesses, creating change, and proving that strength and vulnerability go hand in hand. Sarasota is just one chapter of that story, but what a powerful chapter it is.

## Why Sarasota?

Sarasota is more than a beautiful beach town—it's a city with a rich history of reinvention and ambition. Once known primarily as the winter home of the Ringling Bros. Circus, Sarasota has evolved into one of the fastest-growing metropolitan areas in Florida, with a population that has surged past 800,000. It's a hotspot for entrepreneurs, a cultural hub with a thriving arts scene, and a place where innovation meets opportunity.

Women, in particular, have been at the forefront of this growth. Sarasota boasts one of the highest percentages of women-owned businesses in Florida, with female entrepreneurs leading industries from real estate to wellness to tech. Philanthropy is also deeply woven into the fabric of the community, with women heading some of the region's most impactful nonprofits, from arts education to social services.

And then, of course, there's the Sarasota spirit—the sense of community, the drive to create, the desire to build something lasting. The women in this book aren't just thriving here; they're making Sarasota better—more inclusive, more dynamic, more full of possibility.

## The Women of Sarasota: Stories That Inspire

Every woman in this book has a story that could stop you in your tracks. Not because they followed some perfect, linear path to success, but because they fought for their place in the world—through challenges most people never see.

There's Nazare Edelson, who had to rebuild her entire life after an unexpected divorce left her with no degree, no career, and no clear way forward. Instead of letting fear define her, she rose—one step at a time—turning her challenges into a career that not only supports her family but allows her to help others find their place in Sarasota, too.

Then there's Cathy Bryant, a woman who turned unimaginable loss into action. When her best friend was taken from her in an act of domestic violence, she could have let grief consume her. Instead, she channeled it into a mission, creating a nonprofit that restores dignity to people rebuilding their lives—because no one should have to do it alone.

And Amber Gingerich, who thought she was just starting a small business selling secondhand baby clothes, only to realize she was creating something much bigger. When she endured the devastating loss of two babies, it was the very moms she had built a community around who held her up. What started as a business became a sisterhood—one that proves true connection is about more than just what we buy and sell.

These stories aren't just about business. They're about resilience. Reinvention. The power of showing up—not just for ourselves, but for each other.

## Why This Matters

If we only tell the polished version of success, we do a disservice to every woman out there struggling to find her way. The truth is, the path to success is rarely straight. It's messy. It's full of detours, setbacks, and moments where you question everything.

But these women? They kept going. And by sharing their stories, they're lighting the way for others.

That's the heart of *Slaying Sarasota*. It's not just a book—it's a movement. A space where women's voices are heard, where their journeys are honored, and where their strength is celebrated.

## A Movement, Not Just a Book

From *Slaying Southwest Florida* to *Slaying Nashville* to *Slaying Atlanta*, this series exists to lift up women's voices in cities across the country. Each book is a love letter to the women who make a place what it is. And if Sarasota is any indication, the future is fierce, resilient, and deeply connected.

So as you read these pages, I hope you find inspiration. I hope you see yourself in these stories. And most of all, I hope you remember this:

Your story matters too.

Welcome to *Slaying Sarasota*. Let's begin.

# Beauty Within

## Genesis Krick

Genesis Hey Krick, M.A., CLC, is a dynamic high-performance strategist, executive business coach, and the founder and CEO of Dream Ignite Build. With over a decade of experience, Genesis is passionate about empowering high-achieving women—entrepreneurs, moms, and executives—to unlock their fullest potential, elevate their businesses, and create balance in both their personal and professional lives.

As a high-performance expert, Genesis works with clients who are ready to scale their businesses, break through barriers, and achieve extraordinary success without sacrificing their well-being. Her strategic approach combines mindset, energy management, and sustainable systems to help individuals perform at their best while maintaining a grounded and fulfilling life.

Genesis is also a bestselling author, having written and contributed to five books, including *Unleash Your Potential* and *Slaying Tampa Bay*. A sought-after speaker and media personality, she has been featured on ABC7, Atlanta57, BLOOM TV, and Fox13, sharing her insights on leadership, productivity, and personal growth.

Known for her inspiring approach and hands-on coaching, Genesis is dedicated to guiding women through transformational growth, helping them step into their power and create lasting impact in their careers and lives. When she's not working with clients, Genesis enjoys spending time with her husband and four children, writing, and planning her next adventure over an Americano and cake pops.

www.instagram.com/genesisheykrick
www.linkedin.com/genesisheykrick
www.youtube.com/@dreamignitebuild
www.facebook.com/genesisspeaks
www.genesisspeaks.com

——

When we're young, the world feels like it's full of infinite possibilities. We dream of making our mark, and the desire to be someone significant grows stronger. As an independent young girl, I always knew I wanted to leave a legacy, but along the way, I fell into circles that made me believe I had to change who I was to be accepted and valued. I thought I had to conform to society's standards of beauty to be appreciated.

After having four children and nursing each of them, my body changed in ways I wasn't expecting. Aging, too, wasn't an idea I embraced with open arms. I considered getting breast implants as a way of turning back the clock. If I could do it, why not? My husband and I discussed it, and I decided it made sense at the time.

But beauty is far more than what we see on the outside. It's merely a shell for what truly shines from within. The way we give, serve, communicate, and connect with others is what defines our beauty. Going through breast implant illness (BII) and experiencing the debilitating symptoms firsthand was a wake-up call. It forced me to realize how much I had wanted to be something I wasn't, and how that desire affected my health in ways I didn't understand at the time.

It all started one day at Burn Boot Camp. I had always thrived on high-intensity workouts—jumping, running, heavy lifting, and pushing my heart rate. But during my warm-up, something unusual happened: I felt a sharp pain in the arch of my left foot. At first, I dismissed it, but deep down, I knew something wasn't right. Almost instinctively, I thought, *this could be breast implant illness.* It seemed absurd to me at the time. How could something affecting my breasts have anything to do with my foot? As a passionate runner, this was terrifying. Running marathons, 5Ks, and everything in between has always been a source of clarity for me. The thought that this injury could stop me from doing what I loved was hard to accept.

What followed was a long and painful health journey. At first, I thought it was a sprain and tried to push through the pain. Eight months later, it had worsened. I could barely walk normally, was constantly fatigued, and started noticing strange rashes on my body. My muscles ached, and I felt like I couldn't do everyday activities. Thoughts of "Will I be able to keep up with my kids?" and "Will I ever be able to work out the way I used to?" raced through my mind. I felt as if my body was falling apart. It's true what they say—our minds can be stronger than our bodies, and I had always lived by that mantra. Whether running a race or waking up for the tenth time with my kids in the middle of the night, I pushed myself mentally. But this time, I had to dig deeper and understand the root of the issue.

I did something I now regret. Despite the pain, I chose to run a half marathon I had signed up for, determined that "nothing would stop me." But in hindsight, I should have listened to my body. I ran it hard, ignoring the pain in my foot and knee. The second half of the race was almost unbearable. When I crossed the finish line, relief flooded me, but walking became a struggle. A few weeks later, I saw an orthopedic surgeon who diagnosed me with a collapsed arch and stress fracture. He looked at me and said, "You will never run again," I stared at him in disbelief and instantly broke down in tears. He looked at me with sad eyes and said, I'm sorry...I had no words, only an overwhelming sense of sadness. I was immediately fitted with a boot, and for the next four weeks, I was unable to participate in anything the way I wanted to. It was frustrating, and it felt debilitating. I couldn't exercise, couldn't do the things that brought me joy.

When I was finally able to remove the boot, I felt a deep sense of gratitude. It's only when we lose the ability to do the simple things we take for granted that we realize how much we miss. That day marked a turning point for me. I began asking myself: *What will it take for me to prioritize longevity?* I needed to reassess my goals and focus on what truly mattered. I wanted to show up for my family and for life in the best possible way. To do that, I had to reevaluate my habits and choose the activities that would foster long-term health and well-being.

As I dove into research, I learned that many of the symptoms I had been experiencing were linked to breast implant illness. I was shocked. How could this be happening to me? The problem with BII is that it shares symptoms with so many other conditions, making it difficult to identify. On top of that, I had been diagnosed with an underactive thyroid at 12, which later developed into Hashimoto's disease. BII had made my autoimmune symptoms worse and led to other health issues I had never encountered before.

After countless hours of research and discussions with support groups, I made the difficult but necessary decision to remove my implants. I had only had them for three-and-a-half years, but I knew without a doubt it was the right choice. Why keep a foreign object in my body when I was certain it was causing health problems? I shared my decision with my husband and my mom, who decided to come to my home and support me through the surgery. Her unwavering support meant the world to me. After the surgery, I felt an immediate sense of relief, a sense that I had taken a stand for my health and well-being.

I reflected on why I had gotten the implants in the first place—to feel more feminine, youthful, and vibrant. But I soon realized that these were just self-conscious beliefs, shaped by societal pressures. The implants didn't define my worth. I am who I am, wonderfully created by God, and I am forever grateful for the life I've been given.

Through this journey, I've learned that true self-love is about accepting and loving ourselves without enhancements. It's recognizing that our worth isn't based on how we look, but on what's in our hearts. Since removing the implants, I feel a profound sense of connection with myself. My heart feels fuller, and when I touch my chest, I feel my own heartbeat. I can lay on my stomach without discomfort, and I no longer feel self-conscious in family settings. I'm focused on being true to myself.

While I'm still working through some physical pain, I've learned that every challenge holds a lesson. There is growth in every struggle, and I am confident that my decision to remove the implants was the right one. I know that each day will bring more healing, and I believe in the power of positive self-talk and self-love to guide me through it.

Now, my mission is to advocate for women's health. I want to encourage women to look in the mirror and recognize their inner beauty. I hope to inspire them to embrace what truly lights them up which, in turn, allows them to pursue endeavors that promote positivity and self-love. True transformation starts by looking within and asking ourselves what we need at any given moment. Building a support system of like-minded individuals can make all the difference, helping women thrive despite self-doubt and limiting beliefs. My hope is to be an example of how women can rediscover and love themselves, just as they are.

# From Runway to Resilience: The Journey of a Model Turned Entrepreneur and Wellness Advocate

## Kim Broder

Kim Broder is an entrepreneur, children's author, and wellness advocate who inspires others to embrace self-care and personal growth. Raised in a small Fort Lauderdale, Fla., suburb, Kim spent her early years cultivating creativity and resilience as one of five siblings.

At 18, she pursued her dream of modeling, leading to a decade-long career in commercials, print ads, and international pageant competitions. After moving to Los Angeles and later returning to South Florida, Kim transitioned into business, helping her husband Jon run his company, Vortex Legal.

Fueled by her passion for wellness, Kim earned a bachelor's in health science and a master's in health education, and is pursuing a doctorate in healthcare administration. She combined her academic background with her love of self-care to launch Chic Spa in Sarasota, a boutique spa dedicated to helping clients rejuvenate their minds, bodies, and souls. Partnering with her sister Brooke, Kim has built a business that prioritizes elegance, innovation, and community engagement.

Kim is also the creator of *The Bunny Trail* series, a collection of children's books teaching gratitude, kindness, healthy habits, and mindfulness.

Today, Kim balances entrepreneurship, family life with her husband and daughter, and a renewed modeling career. Her life's mission is to inspire women to pursue their passions and embrace wellness at any stage of life. Whether through Chic Spa or her books, Kim's work reflects her belief that self-care and kindness can transform lives.

https://www.instagram.com/kim_kingsbury_broder
www.chic-spa.com
www.thebunnytrailseries.com

———

I grew up in a small suburb outside of Fort Lauderdale, a city where time seems to stand still, and every visit home still feels exactly as it did in my childhood. I am one of five kids, and our childhood lacked cell phones and Wi-Fi, which I couldn't be more grateful for.

When I turned 18, my ultimate goal was to become a model or actress. My determination led me on a 10-year journey of becoming exactly that: a full-time commercial model. I did countless commercials, print ads, and calendars. At the time, Miami was still offering film incentives, so there were many television shows and films being produced in South Florida.

When I was about 23, I decided I wanted to pivot in the industry, so I did just that. I connected with an agency called "Tropic Beauty "(formally known as "Hawaiian Tropic") and started modeling for them. This entailed quite a bit of travel and participating in pageant-like competitions. Thus, I became immersed in a new world: the bikini model and pageant world.

This led to representing Fort Lauderdale in the Miss Swimsuit USA world finals, which, in turn, led to many other doors opening up. I was working and traveling for work more than ever. The next step was obvious; I moved to Los Angeles, Calif. It only took about a year to realize I wanted to move back to South Florida, and so I did. This led to the next chapter in my life: marriage to a wonderful man, Jon. We met at a restaurant on my birthday, and instantly, we became inseparable. About two months after meeting, I moved in with him.

I was 28 years old when we got married, and I wanted to retire from the modeling industry. I started working full-time at my husband's company, Vortex Legal (a legal recruiting firm), helping his accountant and doing marketing. This experience taught me many great business skills I had not learned at my prior jobs. We went to many conferences and networking events for his company, which is where I learned the importance of relationships and the value in the business world of simply showing up.

Around this time, I embraced a spiritual journey, as most people do at some point in their lives. I started going to meditation retreats and educating myself by reading every self-help and spiritual book imaginable. This led to my next endeavor: creating four children's books called *The Bunny Trail* series.

In the first book of *The Bunny Trail* series, I wanted to teach the importance of gratitude. The adventures of Giselle and her family are designed to inspire and enrich the lives of children as they play the "Gratitude Game." This game reminds them to be grateful for all the wonderful people and events in their lives. The stories also inspire kids to make positive choices and feel confident in their abilities.

In the second book, *The Bunnies Go to Europe*, my main goal was to teach the importance of being kind. I created a game called "The Kindness Game." This book in *The Bunny Trail* series teaches children that everyone responds to kindness. It also emphasizes that speaking kindly to others helps create a more harmonious world. As the bunnies travel around Europe, they learn words of kindness in the language of each country they visit. *The Bunnies Go to Europe* explores meaningful concepts that will inspire children to learn more about themselves and the world around them.

The third book in The Bunny Trail series is called *The Bunny Trail for Healthy Kids*. This book is designed to educate, entertain, and encourage parents and their children to adopt positive lifestyle habits. Kids will be happier and have more energy for play and learning when they:

- Eat fresh, organic food, including fruits and vegetables
- Play outside in the fresh air and sunshine
- Spend less time watching television, playing video games, and talking and texting on their cellphones.

Most importantly, this bunny book supports parents and their children in creating more family togetherness by playing the "Best Part of the Day" game, which means putting away phones, video games, and tablets at the dinner table and sharing about the day with each other.

The final book in the series is *The Bunnies Learn to Meditate*. The goal of this book is simple. It teaches parents how to get their kids interested in meditation at an early age. Meditation can help anyone (including kids) relax and let go of stress.

Eventually, we moved to Sarasota, I decided to finish school and eventually earned a bachelor of arts in health science, and a master's degree in health education. I wanted to combine my personal passion for self-care with my experience and education, so I decided to open and operate a spa. I taught myself everything about the industry. Chic Spa is my passion project. I do it because I truly believe massage is a great way to heal your mind, body, and soul. It's important to take time for yourself to relax and rejuvenate, and massage is an excellent way to do it.

## Why Chic Spa is so Special

What sets Chic Spa apart is its unwavering commitment to elegance and style, which is epitomized by its name. But beyond aesthetics, Chic Spa prides itself on its constant evolution and dedication to excellence. My ultimate goal is the pursuit of innovation, which ensures that clients are treated to a range of massage techniques and services designed to fully reset the mind, body, and soul.

I believe that true fulfillment lies in witnessing the transformative power of self-care. Whether it's relieving pain or simply offering a moment of respite from the demands of the world, Chic Spa's mission is to nurture the well-being of its clients both within its walls and in the comfort of their homes.

In addition to my BA and master's degrees, I am currently working on my doctorate in healthcare administration, while also taking care of my baby Aria, who is one year, five months old and growing!

## Community Engagement in Sarasota

As a part of the Sarasota community, I find ways to network for Chic Spa and to connect with like-minded women who have similar interests in the wellness industry and learn how to incorporate all of my passions, educational background, and experience, while building relationships around them.

I have grown to love Sarasota and have such a personal connection to the city and gratitude for discovering such a beautiful place to live where I share my passion of overall well-being within the community.

## My Life Beyond Work

When I am not dedicating my time to Chic Spa and creating new ways to expand and pivot my business, I try to spend every moment with friends and family, enjoying my life as much as possible.

Boating along the serene waters of Sarasota serves as my personal oasis, offering a refreshing escape from the demands of being an entrepreneur, mom, and student.

I find joy in the simple pleasures of family life, cherishing every moment spent with my husband Jon, our daughter, and our dogs. These cherished moments rejuvenate my spirit and also serve as a reminder of the importance of balance and self-care in maintaining overall well-being.

## Looking Forward

I recently decided to get back into the modeling industry after my daughter turned one and have been doing commercial jobs when I'm not working at the spa or at school.

The beauty of this is that I have so much experience in the modeling industry that I have the freedom to only pick jobs that resonate with me. Somehow, I juggle it all each and every day.

I truly want to inspire all women, not just moms. We can still go to school. We can still run our own businesses. And if we want to, we can still be models in our thirties!

# Slaying Sarasota: A Story of Love, Loss, and Resilience

## Cathy Bryant

Cathy Bryant is a trauma-informed advocate, certified yoga instructor, and co-executive director of Streets of Paradise, a nonprofit dedicated to restoring dignity and creating sustainable communities through disaster relief and purposeful relationships. With roots in rape and domestic violence crisis response, Cathy has spent her life championing safety, empowerment, and support for those facing life's most difficult challenges.

Cathy's work is inspired by her belief in the transformative power of shared stories and the strength found in women supporting women. She has dedicated her career to fostering resilience, advocating for marginalized communities, and building systems of care that provide both immediate relief and long-term stability. As a leader in disaster relief, she has helped countless individuals recover from homelessness, natural disasters, and foster care transitions, ensuring they are met with compassion and tangible support.

Through her yoga practice, Cathy brings mindfulness and balance into her work, emphasizing the healing power of connection and vulnerability. Her leadership is guided by the Streets of Paradise motto, LoveActRepeat—a reminder that love drives action and consistent action creates lasting change.

Deeply committed to empowering women and amplifying their voices, Cathy's life and work are a testament to the strength of community and the enduring impact of advocacy. Whether responding to crises, teaching yoga, or leading disaster relief efforts, Cathy's mission remains the same: to build purposeful relationships and create spaces where everyone can rebuild and rise.

https://www.facebook.com/cathy.bryant.75
https://www.instagram.com/cbryant1707
https://www.threads.net/@cbryant1707

————

When I was asked to contribute a chapter to *Slaying Sarasota*, I knew immediately that my drive to participate came from a desire to be part of a fierce collaboration of women. Two of the women who built me—shaping the core of who I am—were Treva, my best friend from birth until her tragic death, and my daughter, Danielle, whose life-changing illness reshaped my trajectory. Both profoundly influenced my life, leaving me with lessons on grief, hope, and the enduring power of love. This chapter is a tribute to them and the journey they set me on.

## A Friendship Written in the Stars

Treva was more than a best friend—she was my sister in every sense but blood. We grew up side by side, spending countless Sundays at church and summers at church camp. Those shared moments gave us laughter, connection, and a sense of belonging. Treva's quiet strength was something I admired deeply, even as I began to understand the struggles she carried.

As we grew older, life became more complicated. Treva survived an abusive relationship, rebuilding her life with remarkable resilience. She remarried, trusting in love again. Yet, her new husband turned that trust into betrayal, using the safety plan I had written for her—meant to protect her—to orchestrate her death. That parking lot, where she should have been safe, became the site of her murder. The guilt was unbearable. I replayed every decision, every word, searching for what I missed, even though I knew deep down the fault wasn't mine.

Her death didn't just take Treva; it shattered my faith in myself. I left crisis work, feeling incapable and broken. For years, I grieved her absence and the version of myself that died with her. But grief, in its relentless way, eventually taught me to transform that pain into purpose. Streets of Paradise became my way to honor Treva's memory, ensuring that others could find safety and dignity where she could not.

## The Complex Bond of Motherhood

Danielle was strong-willed and difficult from the very beginning. She challenged me in ways I wasn't prepared for, and to be honest, we didn't bond easily in those early years. But when she fell ill at the age of five, everything changed. Her condition—rare, debilitating, and isolating—forced us into an uncharted world of medical care and survival.

Friends and family pulled away, their absence cloaked in judgment and fear. Some in the church believed her illness was a punishment—for a lack of faith, for imagined sins, or perhaps for my failures as a mother. At the same time, my parents' marriage fell apart, and the weight of caregiving felt unbearable. I was left to navigate her care alone, through sleepless nights by her hospital bed and endless days fighting for answers from specialists.

In the midst of all this, something unexpected happened. Danielle's illness became the bridge that brought us together. Her resilience and defiance in the face of her condition showed me a depth of courage I hadn't recognized in her before. She became my teacher, showing me how to fight with everything I had. Through her, I learned that while love cannot always heal, it sustains. It bridges the gap between what is lost and what still remains.

At the same time, losing our community during Danielle's illness planted the seeds of a new passion in me. I began to see the power of creating sustainable, vital communities—ones where people could belong, be supported, and find purpose together. The idea of building something purposeful took root, even as my own world seemed to crumble.

## Building Streets of Paradise

The foundation of Streets of Paradise is built on the lessons Treva and Danielle taught me: that people need safety, dignity, and connection. What began as providing meals and showers for those in need grew into something far greater. Today, we furnish homes for people rebuilding their lives—whether from homelessness, foster care, or disaster. Every item we place— every bed, table, or set of dishes—is an act of restoration, a small piece of stability.

But this work has always been about more than physical necessities. It is rooted in the power of shared stories. When people feel seen and heard, empathy grows. And with empathy, hope takes root. Each interaction—whether furnishing a home or serving a meal—reminds us of our shared humanity.

Even before Streets of Paradise had a name, we were stepping into gaps left by failing systems. Marginalized communities were often excluded from aid, their suffering overlooked. We moved into those forgotten spaces, delivering thousands of meals, showers, and furnishings. These moments were not just acts of service; they were declarations that every life matters.

This mission is guided by our motto: *Love~Act~Repeat.* Love is the heartbeat of our work, informing every decision we make. Action ensures that this love is transformed into tangible support. And repetition reminds us of the persistence required to meet the unending needs of our community. It's a rhythm that drives everything we do, weaving resilience into the fabric of each life we touch.

Grief, however, is a constant companion in this work. It reminds us that we don't only mourn the people we lose; we also mourn the versions of ourselves that are gone. The person I was before Treva's death, before Danielle's illness, no longer exists. But in that loss, I have found strength to rebuild—to reshape those jagged pieces into something meaningful.

**Lessons in Grief and Resilience**

Grief is a paradox: it destroys, but it also transforms. Treva's death and Danielle's illness dismantled my world, forcing me to find new ways to exist. Love, I've learned, is not a shield against pain but the thread that stitches us back together. It is what makes survival possible.

I remember standing in the eye of a hurricane, the air heavy with an unnatural stillness. The storm raged around me, yet in that moment, there was silence. It mirrored the fragile peace I've carried through life's chaos. I have learned to live in that tension—between the calm and the storm, between the broken and the whole.

We grieve not just for those we lose, but for the innocence and certainty that vanish with them. Yet, grief also holds the potential for something beautiful. In the shattered pieces of our lives, there is light. There is the chance to rebuild, to create something new.

## A Call to Vulnerability

This story is not just mine; it belongs to all of us who carry grief and love in equal measure. My hope is that by sharing it, others will feel less alone. Vulnerability is not weakness; it is strength. It is the courage to connect, to act, and to hope.

Treva's passion and Danielle's resilience live on in every meal served, every home furnished, every story shared. Together, we can face life's storms—not unscathed, but unbroken.

Let us be bold enough to share our stories and strong enough to hold space for others. Let us rebuild not only what was lost but what is possible. This is our anthem. This is Streets of Paradise. Love~Act~Repeat.

# Happy, Healthy, and Wealthy in Mind, Body and Soul

### Carolyn Carino

Born and raised outside of Philadelphia, Pa., in Bucks County, Carolyn had an amazing childhood. She still talks with her best friends since first grade every day. From an early age she always embraced inclusiveness. Everyone is a friend.

Right out of high school, she realized "home" looked like opioids, pregnancy, or jail, so she chose to move her life to Sarasota, Fla., in 2008. Stepping into the service industry allowed her to access the absolutely beautiful, kind, and welcoming people of this Suncoast town. Everything happens for a reason. As she embraced Sarasota and all it has to offer, she grew as an adult into who she is today.

Today, Carolyn can celebrate accomplishments such as being a mother of two incredibly innovative and outgoing kiddos; top 20% in her real estate brokerage, Keller Williams on the Water Sarasota, year after year; team lead and founder of The Link Real Estate Group; top 12 Realtors in Sarasota 2023 in *SRQ Magazine*; agent leadership council member at Keller Williams Realty for three years; Women Who Roar in 2024 nominee; BNI member since 2016; president of BNI Chapter Professional Biz Connections 2024–2025; founder of The Link Community Foundation in 2023; founder of The Purge Community Event; founder of The Link Market; and previous owner/operator of Flippin' Fun Gymnastics Adventures, plus many more innovative community connecting events.

Having gone through intense life lessons, Carolyn chooses to believe in a higher power and purpose to drive her to give to others. Today, Carolyn shares her love for this community with many local events, including The Purge Community Event. Using real estate as a conduit to helping others... "Money is good for the good it can do..." She started The Link Community foundation in 2023 to raise funds to be able to grow and build her vision to connect this community and many others.

https://www.instagram.com/carolyncarinothelink/
https://www.facebook.com/carolyn.sproehnle
https://www.facebook.com/CarolynSellsSarasota/
https://linktoallthings.kw.com/
https://thelinkcommunityfoundation.org/

———

After filing for divorce in late 2022, my life seemed to fall apart. Quite honestly, I don't remember much of the beginning of 2023. In August of 2023, I was having fun, deep conversations with friends at a pool and found my faith. I've always been a believer in something bigger, I just never knew what. I continue to learn every day. I knew everything happened for a reason and that reason is not always known at the time. Believing that "it isn't up to me, it happened because it was meant to be," gave (and gives) me the ability to let go of my anxiety and gloom.

God has me.

My angels have me.

Since my awakening, I have seen and talked to God and my angels. I have met my angel. Her name is Mira. She has curly hair and glasses, and reminds me of the girl from the movie *Encanto*, Mirabel. Whether times are tough or amazing, I talk to my angels for guidance.

God is real.

Manifestation is real.

My daily mantra is, "I am open to all good things in abundance. Money flows to me like a river. I am happy, healthy and wealthy in mind, body, and soul."

To have a successful, happy, and fulfilled life, and to get through the hard times, I have discovered that you MUST do a few things.

**Trust in God, however you see your God.**

I personally don't see a person when I think of God. I see a visible wind that spreads slowly and connects absolutely everything. God is the beautiful river, the fish swimming, the pen I write with and the air we all breathe. Knowing and trusting in our higher power will inevitably give us grace in decision making, ease through tough times and the happiest of times.

**Be grateful.**

Thank God for your messy house, your car accident, your marriage, your divorce, your love, and your happiness. Always in all things. When you can shift your mindset to being grateful even when it's hard, the "hard things" will gradually lessen, and you'll live a happier, lighter, calmer existence.

**Give love.**

Give love to everyone and everything. We are each put on this earth to learn this human existence. Make it a good one. Every day I tell my children, "Make someone smile today." What would our world look like if everyone had a smile on their face because another human purposely wanted them to experience love at that moment? You never know what someone is going through. Why not be a positive part of their day? It is a ripple effect. Do you know those people shopping at the grocery store who look so sad and annoyed? I challenge you to make eye contact and smile at them. You just changed their life.

Not quite understanding the power of connection fully, yet always offering love made me "network" and show up as trustworthy while meeting others during my service industry days. This groomed me for my own mobile gymnastics company and career in real estate. Seeing the joy on people's faces makes me so happy. Going through difficult transitions, giving as much positive energy as possible, and seeing a successful outcome is an incredible feeling.

My daughter was born in 2015 while I was running Flippin' Fun Gymnastics Adventures. Bringing children a gymnastics experience, I traveled around to different schools, summer camps and birthday parties. Although a very difficult decision, the heavy lifting involved while working with the apparatus and children gave way for my new career as a realtor. My wonderful mother was in real estate at the time and encouraged me to get my license and help her out. I soon realized real estate melded my love for people and entrepreneurship and stuck with it.

Simultaneously, when I had my daughter, I realized many of my friends were either pregnant or had babies very close to when I had mine. I decided to start a Facebook group called "2015–2016 Sarasota Babies" for everyone to keep in touch. After all, it takes a village, and we were about to go through the similar experiences, whether good or bad. Growth spurts, teething, potty training, and eventually entering school, sports, and so much more. Little did I know, I was creating a space for friendships to form and lasting connections to happen. I put together events every month to get the parents and kids to bond. We got together for holiday parties, trick or treating at assisting living facilities, laying flowers at the Sarasota Veteran's Cemetery on Memorial Day, scavenger hunts and simple playdates at a nearby park. On several occasions, moms would say, "I have size 4t clothes if anyone needs them, and I'm looking for 5t clothes." And so, The Purge was born!

The Purge Community Event started at Colonial Oaks Park in Sarasota with about 10 people. The idea was that everyone "purged" their homes and brought items they no longer needed, such as clothes, toys, shoes, and small housewares. We then set everything up on tables at the park according to categories, and anyone could come and take what they needed/wanted for free.

I remember vividly going to the other random people at the park and telling them to come take things. They were so confused but they happily walked away with some free items for their children and household. Fast forward to now, and we've hosted several successful Purge Community events serving around 400 people each. We now offer free fun (a bounce house), free haircuts, and free food.

Building up this community is my passion. Each person who donates must also place their items in the right categories, further embracing the "community spirit" and helping their neighbors. All of the leftover items are donated to local nonprofits in our area in need of clothing and household items.

From the expanded Purge Event grew the need for funds and a larger vision. The Link Community Foundation was formed in 2023, a 501(c)(3), to be able to fundraise for more Purge Events and save for the future. The foundation is furthering the mission to provide free resources and essential needs, free courses in financial literacy, parenting and advocacy, and future single-parent housing. This is currently in Sarasota, and my goal is to eventually turn this fantastic nonprofit into a National Purge Day, inspiring other towns to give back, create community, and build a brighter future.

Live your life romanticized, like a fairytale or a Hallmark movie, and give as much good as you can. We all go through tough times. Some more than others. We all have those bad days and even weeks. I read a quote once that said, "You can have a bad day, even a bad week, but NEVER allow for a bad month." I live by this. The dark times in my life go much deeper than this chapter. I want to share with you that even if this is you... there is a brighter tomorrow. It's up to YOU to do whatever you choose to be and do in this life. You must see yourself there. Use the three rules from above and I promise you, you will thrive. Go make someone smile today.

# Always Remember to Sparkle

## Loli DiSanto

Loli is a full-time artist celebrated for creating dazzling, three-dimensional sculptures that bring joy and inspiration to homes. With collections featured in galleries across the United States, her art combines bold colors, intricate craftsmanship, and a signature "touch" of sparkle. But beyond the color and crystal-encrusted details lies a deeper purpose: Loli wants to be remembered as someone who truly sparkles from within.

Born and raised in Chicago, Ill., Loli spent her early years as a competitive figure skater, which first ignited her love for all things luminous. After earning a degree in physiology from Michigan State University and graduating from Midwestern University as a physician assistant, she discovered her passion for art later in life. Following a move to Florida in 2013 with her husband and two children, Loli immersed herself in art education, exploring workshops, private lessons, and self-discovery through creative expression.

Her work, often described as "jewelry for the home," reflects her belief that beauty on the outside should resonate with the light within. While the sparkle of her sculptures captures the eye, Loli hopes her legacy will shine through the impact she has on others. She inspires those around her to dream boldly, embrace creativity, and cultivate an inner brilliance that matches the radiance they share with the world. In her words, "Always remember to SPARKLE! You can sparkle on the outside all you want, but what truly matters is the beautiful person who shines from within."

@loli_disanto_artist

www.lolidisanto.com

———

For as long as I can remember, my life was built around helping others. My path as a physician assistant was rooted in a love for science, a commitment to healing, and a deep passion for supporting people through life's challenges. I found immense fulfillment in this work; each day brought a sense of purpose and connection. But as life evolved—through marriage, children, and a move to sunny Florida—I began to feel a subtle pull in an entirely new direction, one I hadn't expected.

The catalyst for this shift was something completely unexpected: art. What began as a casual interest in gallery visits soon blossomed into a fascination. The colors, textures, and forms in each piece spoke to me, as if they each held a story waiting to be uncovered. Driven by this new curiosity, I signed up for my first art workshop. From that point on, art became more than just a pastime—it became a language that allowed me to express parts of myself I hadn't fully explored.

My curiosity soon became a passion. I devoured books on art history and theories of color and form, and each page seemed to open new worlds. I wanted to understand the "why" and the "how" behind every brushstroke, every choice of color, every layered meaning. So, I threw myself into learning. I took classes, attended workshops, and sought to see the world through an artist's eyes. What I discovered was that art wasn't just about technique; it was about capturing something essential and meaningful—something that resonated not just on the canvas but within myself.

One of the most transformative parts of this journey was meeting my mentor, an accomplished artist who guided me through new techniques, helped refine my style, and offered challenges that stretched my boundaries. With each assignment, I felt my understanding deepen, and yet, almost instinctively, I kept reaching for materials that added a hint of sparkle: gold leaf, crystals, shimmering embellishments that seemed to echo back to my childhood as a competitive figure skater, when everything glittered and shined.

The glimmering world of figure skating held a special kind of magic for me. As a child, I was entranced by the sparkle of costumes under the rink lights, the sound of my skates carving into the ice, and the delicate choreography that felt like art in motion. I loved every detail: the rhinestones, the sequins, the way a well-placed crystal could catch the light and turn an ordinary costume into something spectacular. There was a sense of transformation each time I stepped onto the ice—a feeling that anything was possible when surrounded by that dazzling brilliance. That passion for shimmer and shine lingered long after my skating days ended, quietly waiting to resurface in another form.

At first, my mentor gently steered me back to the basics, encouraging me to focus on traditional methods and master foundational techniques. But over time, he began to notice my continual pull toward embellishment. One day, he looked at me with a smile and said, "Just go for it. Do what feels natural—listen to your inner voice."

That simple encouragement felt like permission to finally embrace the part of me that craved sparkle and texture. Inspired by Damien Hirst's iconic dot paintings, I created a piece that leaned into my love of bold color, movement, and dimensionality. My work transformed the traditional dot composition into a three-dimensional design, using dome-shaped components painted in vibrant colors and covered in crystals. The piece shimmered and sparkled, inviting light and movement into every angle. When I presented it to my mentor, he studied it with a look of genuine interest and posed a question that would change everything: "What would this look like if you took it off the wall?"

His question planted a seed in my mind, encouraging me to think beyond the confines of a flat canvas. I began to imagine my art as something sculptural and multi-dimensional, something that could be experienced from every perspective. This question ignited my imagination, opening the door to a new way of creating. I started to see my work as something that could exist in three dimensions, and that shift led to the creation of a collection that would become my signature: three-dimensional egg sculptures.

The symbolism of the egg—rich in its associations with rebirth, renewal, and potential—felt like the perfect expression for this new body of work. Each egg combined the elegance and opulence of a Fabergé egg with the sparkle of a Judith Leiber handbag, infused with bold, pop-art-inspired patterns that celebrated color, life, and joy. Layered with thousands of rhinestones, each piece became a symbol of life and transformation, inviting the viewer to look closer and see the facets anew.

Creating these egg sculptures was, in many ways, a process of self-discovery. I found myself reborn in my art, embracing beauty and the courage to reinvent. My eggs weren't just works of art; they embodied the power of rebirth, of embracing one's true vision, and of daring to explore uncharted paths. Each time I placed another rhinestone or added a new layer of color, I felt a sense of possibility, as if my art were a reminder that we are all capable of reinvention.

This journey of transformation has taught me so much—not just about art, but about life itself. One lesson I hold close, and share often with my children, is that it never hurts to ask. Ask yourself what you want. Ask for help, as I did with my mentor. Dare to dream, and have the courage to pursue those dreams— even when they feel unfamiliar. The world is full of doors waiting to be opened, and each question, each moment of curiosity, can lead us somewhere new.

Art has shown me that we are not limited by the paths we start on. Just as an egg symbolizes life emerging anew, we too can emerge, transform, and follow new passions at any stage. Each of my egg sculptures is a celebration of this journey—a reminder that life, like art, is ever-renewing, a constant invitation to discover, grow, and become something new.

When I look back on the path that brought me here, I think of the moments of curiosity, the unexpected questions, and the encouragement that helped me believe in my vision. My journey became more than just creating beautiful sculptures; it became a story of transformation, of learning to trust myself, and finding the courage to reinvent. Life is filled with opportunities to reimagine, reshape, and rebirth ourselves into something beautiful and unexpected.

I hope my work inspires others to explore their own paths of transformation and to find beauty in all the ways we can be reborn. Art has taught me that we can embrace the pieces of our past while allowing room for growth and change. Each creation is a reflection of my own journey—a journey that has taught me to treasure where I've been and to look forward with excitement to where I'm going.

# From Rock Bottom to Rebirth

## Nazare Edelson

At 34, Nazare Edelson faced a life-altering crossroads: her marriage ended, and with it, the life she had built as a stay-at-home wife and mother. She had no education, career, or financial knowledge to lean on—just a small apartment, her two children, and an overwhelming sense of uncertainty. For years, Nazare had focused entirely on creating a stable, loving home, but in doing so, she lost sight of who she was and what she was capable of achieving.

Starting over was terrifying, but it also sparked a fire within her. With faith, family support, and determination, Nazare began to rebuild. She enrolled in school, pursuing a career that allowed her to provide for her children while staying present in their lives. Walking into class as the oldest person in the room and full of doubt wasn't easy, but she kept showing up. Passing her licensing exam wasn't just a professional milestone—it was a personal triumph that proved she could rise above self-doubt and fear.

Through this journey, Nazare's children have been her greatest source of strength and inspiration. They remind her why perseverance matters and encourage her to dream bigger.

Today, Nazare is a proud real estate professional, a devoted mother, and a woman who has reclaimed her voice. Sarasota's vibrant community of women entrepreneurs inspires her daily to keep growing and helping others find their strength. Her story is proof that starting over isn't the end—it's an opportunity to create a life that truly reflects who you are.

https://www.facebook.com/nazare.edelson
https://www.instagram.com/nazare_sarasotarealtor/
https://nazare.livingvogue.com/

———

The first time I truly looked at myself in the mirror after my divorce, I barely recognized the woman staring back.

The reflection showed a person I'd never taken the time to truly know. I wondered if I'd ever be able to see myself as strong and capable again. My eyes were tired, my spirit bruised, but deep down, I felt a spark of something—hope.

I was 34 years old, starting over with nothing—no education, no career, and no sense of identity. The life I had spent years building as a stay-at-home wife and mother had crumbled, leaving me to wonder who I was and how I was ever going to move forward. I married young, embracing my role as a wife and mother with all my heart. My focus was on creating a warm, nurturing environment for my family. My energy went into supporting my husband's endeavors and prioritizing the needs of our children. I believed I was doing what was best for everyone I loved. Our lives were structured and orderly. My role was clear, and I fulfilled it diligently. At the time, I didn't think much about what lay outside those boundaries. My family's world was my world, and I poured myself into making it as comfortable and stable as possible. Having grown up in a childhood filled with chaos and pain, I was determined to create a different reality—a home rooted in love for my children, no matter the cost to myself. But looking back now, I see how much of myself I set aside.

I wonder now if the sacrifices I made were truly necessary or if I'd lost sight of myself somewhere along the way. My intentions were noble, but my execution left no room for me to grow as an individual. The years I spent focused solely on others blinded me to the person I could have become.

Decisions about finances or our future weren't mine to make. My role was to trust and follow, and so I did. When differences of opinion arose, I often found myself retreating. My husband had a way of thinking quickly, talking confidently, and presenting his arguments so convincingly that I doubted myself before I even spoke. Over time, I began to feel that my voice didn't matter—not because anyone told me explicitly, but because I had internalized the idea that I couldn't contribute in the same way. My thoughts felt small and unworthy. I was meant to complement, not lead. There were moments when I wanted to push back, but I didn't know how. I worried I wouldn't say the right thing or that I'd be misunderstood. It seemed easier to stay quiet than to risk being outsmarted. I told myself this was just the way things were.

My silence wasn't a sign of peace—it was a sign of resignation. Each unspoken thought chipped away at my sense of self-worth. I began to believe the lie that my contributions were insignificant.

I began to shrink emotionally. My confidence dwindled as I doubted my own intelligence and abilities. I didn't recognize it at the time, but I was slowly losing pieces of myself. The strong, capable woman I had once envisioned I'd be seemed further and further away. The day I decided my marriage was over, I stood in the doorway of our big, beautiful house, where my husband would remain, holding my two children's hands, and felt the weight of both heartbreak and hope as I walked away from everything I had known toward the small apartment where we would begin again. When my marriage ended, it wasn't just the loss of a relationship or financial stability that shook me—it was the loss of my identity. The version of myself I had built around my family and marriage was gone, and I was left with nothing but questions: Who am I without these roles? What am I capable of on my own?

I didn't know how to answer those questions, but I knew I couldn't ignore them. My journey toward self-discovery was about to begin, even though I was terrified of what I might find.

Navigating even the simplest tasks felt overwhelming. I didn't have the experience or knowledge to handle the basics of running a household independently. The shame of starting over was crushing. I couldn't stop comparing myself to women who seemed to glide through life effortlessly. My social circle was made up of other affluent stay-at-home mothers, women who couldn't fathom the idea of working. When I chose to leave the life we all knew and take on the necessity of a career, I could feel their quiet judgment, as though I had fallen from grace—no longer an equal, but something lesser in their eyes. They were confident, self-sufficient, and unshaken by challenges. Meanwhile, I felt like I was drowning in insecurity, frozen by fear, and haunted by those relentless questions: How did I let this happen? Why didn't I prepare better? What if I fail? Admitting my struggles to my family was challenging. I was embarrassed to tell them how unprepared I felt for life on my own as a single mother. But when I did open up, I was met with nothing but compassion. My family became my lifeline, lifting me up on the days when I couldn't do it myself. Their support reminded me that I wasn't alone, even when the darkness felt suffocating. Still, even with their love and encouragement, the path ahead felt impossibly overwhelming.

Every choice I made seemed to carry the weight of a hundred consequences. I felt as though I was constantly on the verge of making the wrong move, but I knew I couldn't give up.

Every day was a battle against feelings of worthlessness and fear. I felt like I had failed—not just myself, but my children. The guilt was unbearable. But in the midst of all that fear and doubt, one thing became clear to me: I needed to show my children that independence and happiness are vital. I wanted them to see that their value wasn't tied to anyone else's approval or support, but to their own capabilities. I wanted my children to grow up confident in their ability to stand on their own two feet, no matter what life threw at them. They deserved to know that they could dream, achieve, and live life on their terms. And I realized the best way to teach them that was to live it myself. A flicker of determination began to grow. I couldn't let my story end here. I wanted to prove to myself, my children, and let's be honest, even my ex-husband, that I was stronger than my circumstances.

I had spent too many years doubting myself to let fear win now. My children needed a role model, and I was determined to become one.

I began to pray every day—not for all the answers to suddenly appear, but for the courage to take the next step. Slowly, I started piecing my life back together. My first major step was enrolling in school. I needed a career to support myself and my family. Something that allowed me to take them to school and pick them up, attend field trips, and be home if they needed me.

I won't forget the first time walking into class—I felt completely out of place. Not only was I the oldest in the room, but I was surrounded by people who seemed to have their lives together while I struggled to hold mine together. But I kept showing up. I pushed through the fear and self-doubt that whispered I wasn't smart enough or good enough to succeed. Passing my licensing exam was more than just a professional milestone; it was a deeply personal victory. For the first time in years, I achieved something myself. I did it on my own, while still being a mom. That moment was proof that I was capable, even in the face of overwhelming doubt.

Starting a career later in life was humbling. I made mistakes—so many mistakes. I trusted too easily, stayed silent when I should have spoken up, and doubted my instincts far more often than I should have. Those missteps taught me a lesson: that failure isn't final and that my voice matters. With each experience, I found my voice—the one I had silenced for so long. Slowly, I realized that success wasn't about never falling; it was about always getting back up.

My career gave me more than financial stability; it gave me a sense of purpose and independence. Helping families find their dream homes became a way for me to channel my resilience into something meaningful. Through all the highs and lows of this journey, my children have been my greatest source of strength and inspiration. They've cheered me on at every milestone, celebrated every win, and lifted me up when I felt like giving up. Their unwavering belief in me has been my anchor, even on the toughest days. Watching them grow into resilient, compassionate individuals has been the most profound blessing of my life. They are my "why"—the reason I push forward, even when the path feels steep.

I often look at them and feel immense pride, knowing they're growing up witnessing the power of determination and resilience.

No matter what I've achieved professionally, nothing compares to the pride I feel as their mother. Knowing they see me as strong and capable keeps me grounded and reminds me why I started this journey in the first place. Rebuilding my life was about confronting the woman in the mirror—the one carrying years of self-doubt and fear—and learning to see her as enough. I had to unlearn the belief that my worth was tied to my roles as wife and mother. I had to forgive myself for the mistakes I made and the ways I allowed others to define my life. And perhaps most importantly, I had to learn that true strength comes from knowing when to lean on others.

My family, friends, and faith became my safety net. They reminded me that I didn't have to carry the weight of the world on my own. Today, I look back at the woman I once was with immense pride. The journey hasn't been easy, but it has been transformative. I've gone from rags to riches, to rags again, and back to riches—not just financially, but emotionally and spiritually.

I'm no longer the woman who stayed silent or doubted her worth. I've found my voice, my strength, and my purpose. I've learned that success isn't about avoiding failure—it's about learning, growing, and rising stronger each time you fall. I've built a life that reflects who I truly am, and every step of the way, I've carried the lessons of my past with me, using them to fuel my future.

I know now that resilience isn't just surviving—it's thriving despite the obstacles.

Sarasota played a pivotal role in this transformation. Its vibrant community and supportive network of women entrepreneurs inspired me to dream bigger. The city fueled my growth, reminding me that no matter how lost I felt, I was part of something greater.

To the women who feel stuck, lost, or overwhelmed: You are not alone. Starting over is terrifying, but it's also an opportunity to build something extraordinary. You don't need all the answers today. Take one step, then another. Progress, not perfection, will carry you forward. Lean on those who love you, trust yourself, and never forget: You are capable of rewriting your story.

# Discovering my Why and Building a Community, One Onesie at a Time

### Amber Gingerich

Amber Gingerich is a Bradenton, Fla., native who left for college and started her career before moving back home with her husband, Jeff, in 2010. They've been married for 18 years and have four amazing kids—three boys and one girl. Yes, their home is super loud and chaotic! Amber currently homeschools their two youngest, and when she's not teaching or running a business, you can find her at the barn with her daughter, riding their two horses, or cheering on her boys at soccer and baseball games.

She is a follower of Jesus first and foremost, an active member of Oasis Church in Bradenton, and a middle school youth leader. Her faith deeply influences how she connects with others and operates her business.

In 2012, she launched Rhea Lana's of Sarasota as a way to serve local families. What started as a ministry has grown into something far greater. Today, they work with over 500 consigning families and welcome more than 2,500 shoppers to each event. Beyond the numbers, Amber is most proud of the connections they make in the community.

Through Rhea Lana's of Sarasota, she strives to love moms well—meeting them where they are and providing them with a way to earn extra income, afford necessities on a budget, and connect with others in a safe, welcoming space. Whether it's through their events, the team of 60+ moms who work each season, or the nonprofits they partner with, her mission is simple: serve moms with love and integrity.

https://www.facebook.com/RheaLanaSarasota
https://www.instagram.com/rhealanasofsarasota/

———

In 2005, my soon to be husband and I were driving and talking about our future and what it may look like. We both felt the Holy Spirit nudging our hearts, and we had an overwhelming sense that there was some big ministry or service in our future. We had no direction on what this would look like, but we felt it would be important.

Skipping to October of 2011, I was attending a playgroup with my two-year-old son and four-month-old daughter. I was busy chasing my toddler between the ball pit and the bounce house and struggling through some small talk with the other moms. Small talk isn't easy for me; I was trying to make new "mom friends" as we had moved back to the area the year prior and weren't plugged into any social circles. A woman approached me and handed me a postcard inviting me to shop at this new event coming to Manatee County called Rhea Lana's. She had to go out to her car and grab one for me. I wonder what would have happened if she didn't have more postcards? It was a small thing, just a postcard, but it was also a moment that shifted my life in a big way.

A couple of days later I was chatting with my sisters-in-law about Rhea Lana's children's consignment event, wondering if it was something we could do ourselves. A couple months later, my sister-in-law Rachel and I were buying our own franchise in Sarasota. We did not have a clue how to run a business or what it would entail but I did know one thing, God was leading us down a new path.

Being a stay-at-home mom was an answered prayer and a huge blessing, but I craved a new challenge. Before kids, I had worked and put myself through college, and not working outside the home felt a little awkward. This new business sounded like the perfect way to balance being a full-time mom and contributing to our household income. Rachel and I ran the business together for nine years until 2021, when she decided to step away, and I took on full ownership.

Now, when people ask me what I do, I tell them I sell used onesies. Technically this is true, but the reality is about so much more than that—and it's always amusing to watch the confusion and intrigue on people's faces when I say "used onesies"! Launching Rhea Lana's of Sarasota is about building a community of women and being given the chance to support and love moms in Sarasota. Moms initially consign and come to shop, but what they find is a village of women who are walking through motherhood alongside them.

Our first event launched with 50 consignors. Today, we've grown to serve over 500 consigning families. This doesn't happen by just selling onesies; our growth stems from fostering a community of moms who feel supported and seen. It helps moms stretch their budgets, make a little extra cash on their unused children's items, and feel seen and supported. Although, I didn't see the heart of the business clearly in the beginning.

During the early years of Rhea Lana's of Sarasota, as I juggled the demands of growing a business and raising a young family, I began to uncover my "why." My two children were just one and three years old when I discovered I was unexpectedly pregnant with baby number three. The timing felt overwhelming as I was also pouring my energy into our second consignment event, which experienced tremendous growth and was a success.

Shortly after that sale, however, my world shifted. I learned that I had lost our daughter at 17 weeks. I delivered her on November 15, 2012. I struggle to recall memories of the weeks following her birth. Grieving her loss was hard, and it was the beginning of a difficult season in my life. I remember crying and praying for another pregnancy, and my prayers were answered. I became pregnant again as we were planning our third sale. Just weeks before the sale, at 15 weeks pregnant with a little boy, I lost him too. He was delivered on April 1st.

Physically and emotionally broken, I was faced with the task of running a sale surrounded by women and expectant mothers after losing two babies back to back. I had no idea how I would make it through each day, let alone manage a growing sale. As hard as it was, this is the event where I realized the heart behind running an event serving moms. Rhea Lana's isn't just about consigning and shopping; it's about the moms. My pregnancy losses made this clear in ways I couldn't have anticipated.

I've always been the person who wears her emotions on her face, whether I want to or not. During that sale, it was clear to many that I was not okay. Time and again, women approached me with compassion. They saw my pain and poured into me—praying over me, supporting me, and offering words of comfort. They didn't just see a business owner; they saw a hurting mom, and they rallied around me while I grieved.

Toward the end of our sale, I distinctly remember a moment when I was eating dinner and a group of women sat around me.

They shared their stories of pregnancy losses, asked me questions about mine, and asked me the names of the children I had lost. No one had asked that up until that point. These women wanting to know broke me, but in a good way. I walked away from the sale knowing I had a lot of hurt to work through but also knowing that I was going to do all I could to support women in Sarasota, not just by selling onesies, but by creating a space where they felt welcome and safe. No matter our differences, we are moms, and we can love each other right where we are. I realized it was my goal to build my business while loving others well.

While I had finally learned my "why," I understood the purpose behind the business, but balancing work and being a mother didn't become any easier. My life is a constant balancing act, and while I wouldn't trade it for anything, I'll be the first to admit it's really hard.

I've been married for 18 years to an amazing man, and together we're raising four busy kids. Between homeschooling my youngest two, running a business, staying active in our church, and supporting our kids in their passions, some days it feels like I'm barely keeping my head above water.

The truth is, most days my mental load feels overwhelming, and I question if I'm doing a good job at anything. Am I present enough for my kids? Am I making the right decisions for my business? Am I being a good wife?

I'm learning that I can't do everything perfectly, and I'm trying to make peace with that. I continually remind myself, "I am capable of many things but only good at a few." It reminds me to prioritize what matters most—my faith, my family, and finding joy in life.

I think many moms and entrepreneurs can relate to this struggle. We're all trying to do so much, and it's easy to feel like we're falling short. I've come to realize that two of the most important things are grace and the ability to step back and rest. Life is hard, but it's a gift, and I'm trying to embrace the mess.

Rhea Lana's of Sarasota has flourished and grown over the past 13 years, and I've grown as a leader alongside it. I've had the privilege of building a team of incredible women who share my desire to love others well—including some of the same women who poured into me as I sat at that table during my third event.

Is this the "big ministry" my husband and I had imagined back in 2005? I believe it is. It's a joy to serve Sarasota moms and to build something that not only supports families but fosters connection and community.

I see how God used this journey to shape me. From a young 28-year-old who knew so little about running a business, I've grown into a woman who is resilient, compassionate, and willing to take on big challenges through the strength He provides. This business has not only transformed my life but also allowed me to serve others in a meaningful way, fulfilling that nudge I felt all those years ago.

I'm learning to see myself as God does—capable, determined, and loved—and to embrace the joy in the chaos of raising a family while building a business. If there's one thing I want other women to take from my story, it's this: You don't have to have it all figured out to start. Just take that first step in faith and let God do the rest.

# Unpacking Gratitude: How Connections Shape Our Lives

## Dr. Stacie Herrera

Dr. Stacie Herrera is a dynamic force in youth mental health, education, and innovation. As the founder/CEO of Herrera Psychology and Co-Founder of HumanizEDU, she champions psychologically safe environments where young people can thrive. A licensed school psychologist with over two decades in Sarasota County, Dr. Herrera is dedicated to addressing the youth mental health crisis through prevention, psychoeducation, and a systemic approach that emphasizes embracing neurodiversity and individual strengths.

A global partner with the Genius Group and accredited Genius Educator, Dr. Herrera is committed to empowering others to discover their unique purpose. She co-authored *Unpacking Bliss: The Suitcase Theory of Life* and recently developed AI brain coaches available through the website Telement.AI, leveraging technology to expand access to mental health resources.

Dr. Herrera's leadership and contributions have earned her notable recognition, including the Sarasota Chamber of Commerce's 2023 Minority Small Business of the Year Award and multiple accolades from SRQ Magazine in the field of mental health. As JFCS board chair (2024–2026), an Impact 100 Sarasota member, and a recipient of the Opportunities For All Grant, she actively supports community resilience and growth.

A California native from Big Bear Lake, Dr. Herrera has called Sarasota home for 22 years, raising four children in the area. Through her work and advocacy, she continues to inspire meaningful change, empowering individuals and communities to flourish.

https://www.instagram.com/dr_stacie/
https://www.facebook.com/drstacieherrera
https://www.linkedin.com/in/dr-stacie-herrera/

––––

Anxiety storms through my body like a hurricane—chaotic, overwhelming, and relentless. But when I anchor myself in gratitude, the clouds begin to break. My jaw unclenches, my shoulders soften, and my heart slows its panicked pace. In those moments, I rediscover my grounding: the connections that have shaped me, the friendships that sustain me, and the family ties that remind me of resilience. Gratitude doesn't erase the storm, but it creates a calm eye within it.

During the most challenging time of my life, as I navigated the tumultuous waters of divorce from my first husband, my mind was firmly locked on everything that was unraveling. Anxiety had me engulfed, filled with cortisol and tension that resonated throughout my body. It was my sister, Sandi, who reached out to check on me, suggesting I focus on one thing that was going well. My immediate response was raw: "The sun is f@$king shining!" Yet, in that simple acknowledgment, I began to shift my perspective.

Gratitude and anxiety are incompatible; one dissolves the grip of the other. Laughter and genuine connections allow us to weather the toughest storms. When others express their gratitude toward me and the support I've provided, it lifts my spirit, affirming that I've found my sense of purpose. As a child psychologist with a doctorate in school psychology, my profession allows me to feel in flow, utilizing my superpowers of holding space, teaching strategies, and empathically guiding others away from negative thoughts.

In my dual roles as a psychologist and small business owner, I thrive on data, statistics, progress monitoring, and the elusive return on investment. As I prepared for this chapter, I envisioned graphs and charts meant to encourage women business owners and community leaders to assess their own impact and legacy. However, I believe our community truly thrives when we collaborate and rally around a unified cause or vision—much like the remarkable resilience we witness after each hurricane.

So, what if we shifted our focus from quantifying impact through numbers to measuring human connection, gratitude, perseverance, a sense of purpose, supporting others in their time of need, and fostering true belonging?

In August of 2016, I received the most heartfelt note from an 18-year-old client:

"Dr. Stacie, Thank you so much for helping me survive the toughest year of my life so far. It seems like it would have been impossible without you. Thank you for the keen insight and multiple perspectives you brought to every issue I had brought up. And, thank you for keeping me calm and saving my relationship with my mom."

This particular client was a gifted student, a talented musician, and an Eagle Scout who navigated his senior year while simultaneously meeting his therapeutic goals and setbacks, often unnoticed by educators, peers, and mentors. Like many high-achieving youth, he struggled in silence.

I measure my impact in personal connections—how the youth I work with see themselves in a new light, equipped with skills and abilities to navigate life's winding roads. Sometimes it's a celebratory text from a parent when a child meets a therapy goal; other times, it's the look in a client's eyes that conveys renewed confidence and joy. This note, however, holds a special place in my heart because my client and I shared a similar history: growing up in a household shaken by addiction, filled with empty promises and disrupted connections, feeling like "The Parent" at a very young age while navigating adolescence.

In our sessions, I encouraged him to set boundaries and advocate for his needs—even when those needs clashed with his mother's desires. With each breakthrough, I felt a quiet, personal victory. Guiding him was like reaching back through time to my teenage self, offering the tools I once needed to heal. His courage mirrored my own journey, and together we transformed pain into resilience.

When I started graduate school in 2008, my intention was to help others, not fully recognizing that my personal healing journey had just begun. As I delved into different modalities through my program and my own spiritual path, I embraced positive psychology and began to believe that there was sense to the chaos. I knew that becoming a child psychologist was my purpose on this planet. I trusted that the best outcomes would reveal themselves.

After graduating with my doctorate in school psychology in 2013 and spending two years interning in the Sarasota County School District, I found that there wasn't a job waiting for me. I interviewed for a position in the neighboring county but wasn't keen on the commute. A conversation with a local clinical psychologist who specialized in working with children opened an unexpected door. Although she was hesitant about hiring me for a postdoctoral position, she wanted to be helpful. This unique opportunity set me on the path I walk today. Had I stayed in the school system, I might have remained a school psychologist, but instead, I ventured into private practice, and in 2016, I opened Herrera Psychology.

Looking back, I realize the greater impact I've made through private practice. Herrera Psychology serves children and families, and the company I co-founded with my sister, Sandi Herrera, HumanizEDU, provides school-based mental health opportunities as well. Our mission is to create psychologically safe working and learning environments where everyone has the tools to manage life's big emotions and foster connection. Starting my own business was a daunting leap into uncertainty, but what we've built is making a profound ripple in our community.

Perhaps it would have been easier to secure an office job while my children were in school or to remain within the structured schedule of a school district. But I have never been one to take the easy path. My curiosity and desire to learn led me to explore new horizons. By letting go of specific outcomes and focusing instead on the feelings I desired—making an impact, aligning with my values, using my talents, and creating meaningful connections—I embraced a form of quantum thinking that paid off.

One of the most poignant moments in my journey came with that client I mentioned earlier. His grandfather, a proudly engaged and supportive figure, created a village of support around him. In February 2020, his grandfather shared an update:

"His current interest in psychology is in the field of music cognition: how people hear, understand, appreciate, and perform music. Last summer, he lugged six books around with him in that field—not because they were assigned—but because they helped him understand how the mind works in relation to music. In the fall of 2021, my grandson is planning to attend graduate school at one of eight schools, the identity to be revealed at a later date. He wants to continue in psychology and music performance."

I like to think our conversations during his senior year sparked his interest in psychology, extending the ripple of our connection.

Tragically, in November 2020, my client died in a hit-and-run accident.

The news jolted my daily existence, reminding me to deeply connect with each person who crosses my path. The thank you card he wrote became a tangible reminder of our impact on each other's lives. It forced me to reflect on my work and life's purpose, highlighting the profound significance of every connection we make.

Connection is our lifeline, the unseen thread that holds us together in times of joy and sorrow. So, send the thank you card. Share your passion and purpose. Pause to measure your impact not by numbers but by the lives you've touched. Together, we can create ripples of gratitude and belonging that expand far beyond ourselves. Let's commit to staying connected—starting today.

Psychological research underscores the importance of social connections. The U.S. surgeon general has declared that we are living in an epidemic of loneliness:

"Approximately half of U.S. adults report experiencing loneliness, with some of the highest rates among young adults."

A 2022 study found that when people were asked how close they felt to others emotionally, only 39 percent of adults in the United States said they felt very connected to others.

"Time spent engaging with friends, especially among young people aged 15 to 24, has decreased by nearly 70% over almost two decades, from roughly 150 minutes per day in 2003 to 40 minutes per day in 2020."

Even before the pandemic, we were losing connections through busyness, geographic separation, and the replacement of in-person activities with virtual interactions. However, having social connections remains one of the most reliable predictors of a long, healthy, and satisfying life. I encourage you to focus on increasing social connections, fostering genuine relationships, and inquiring about the quality and quantity of social interactions within your sphere of influence.

Here's how we can create a ripple of change together:

- **Stay connected.** Prioritize relationships that nourish your spirit.
- **Send a thank you card.** A simple gesture can strengthen bonds and uplift someone's day.
- **Share your passion and purpose.** Let others see what drives you and inspires them to share theirs.
- **Generate your ripple of impact through gratitude, genuine connection, and humanity.** We are hardwired to band together, and our collective efforts can create profound change.

By embracing these practices, we honor our innate need for connection and contribute to a more compassionate, resilient community. To delve deeper into these concepts and explore strategies for fostering bliss in your life, join me in my upcoming book, *Unpacking Bliss: The Suitcase Theory of Life*, written by the Herrera Sisters, available in April 2025. Let's embark on this journey together, unpacking the essentials for a fulfilled and connected existence.

# Finding My Way Home

## Lauren Hitchen

Lauren Hitchen hails from the charming town of Berwick-upon-Tweed, situated between England and Scotland. At the age of 16, she relocated to Sarasota in 2001 with her entrepreneurial parents but soon returned to the UK without them and her brother. In 2017, Lauren returned to Sarasota, this time with her husband, Jonathan, and their son, Ethan.

Her entrepreneurial journey commenced in 2005 with the establishment of her own cleaning business in Sarasota. When she returned to Sarasota in 2017, she and her brother took over an existing window cleaning company. By 2022, Lauren became a permanent US resident, freeing herself from immigration constraints and allowing her to explore various business opportunities and the freedom to explore the world.

This newfound freedom led her to found Jet Set Travel Group, a venture dedicated to making travel dreams come true while also mentoring aspiring business travel advisors. Lauren and her family travel the globe together, inspiring others to embrace the freedom to explore diverse cultures and experiences.

In early 2024, Lauren teamed up with her friend Catalina to launch Rosa Tierra, an online brand specializing in high-quality clothing sourced from Colombia and other countries in South America. Within three months of its UK launch, Rosa Tierra received acclaim by being featured in *Vanity Fair UK* and rapidly expanded to the United States and beyond. Lauren Hitchen's journey embodies resilience, creativity, and a passion for travel, highlighting her commitment to empowering others to pursue their dreams.

**Clothing brand**

Instagram: @RosaTierra
https://rosatierra.com

**Travel agency**
Instagram: @thejetsetgetaway

**Travel business consultant**

Instagram: @lauren.hitch
https://laurenhitchen.com

––––––

If you had told me as a teenager growing up in a tiny town on the English-Scottish border, that I would one day be living in sunny Sarasota, Fla., running businesses, raising a family, and mentoring others, I would have laughed you right out of the room. Life has a funny way of taking you to places you never imagined, right? Mine has been a journey of twists, turns, and the occasional sharp detour, but every challenge has shaped who I am today—and honestly, I wouldn't change a thing.

I'll never forget when it all began. In 2001, when I was just 16, my parents decided to move our family across the pond to Sarasota. From a quaint little town where everyone knows your name to the bustling beaches and heat of Florida—it was a culture shock, to say the least! I had to adjust quickly, learning to navigate a new world while dealing with homesickness. There were visa and travel restrictions. It made things even trickier, limiting what I could do and where I could travel to, but I soaked in every experience during those difficult eight years. It made me stronger.

Then, in 2007, I took a leap and discovered what I wanted to do: fashion marketing. I was accepted to Parsons College in New York City, but the 2008 economic crash had other plans for me!

By 2008, I had packed my bags and returned to the UK on my own. I was thankful to my aunt and grandparents for helping me find my feet and help me set up my life all over again!

That's when everything changed. I met Jonathan, my husband, in 2011 while working in the hospital, and we fell in love. We got married in Sarasota in 2013—a destination wedding that turned into a bit of a travel-planning extravaganza for me. Coordinating flights and accommodations for over 40 family members from the UK was no small task, but I loved every minute of it. I didn't realize it at the time, but that was the beginning of my love affair with travel planning.

After the wedding, Jonathan and I went back to the UK, and life carried on. I worked agency jobs, gaining experience in networking and adaptability while Jonathan pursued his nursing career. We traveled together whenever we could, dreaming of the life we wanted to build. Then, in 2015, our beautiful son Ethan was born, and parenthood threw us headfirst into a whirlwind of joy, fear, and resilience.

Ethan's birth was complicated, to say the least—a traumatic cesarean section that left me in the hospital for ten days, followed by months of home care for my recovery. Just as we found our feet as new parents, Ethan started having health challenges of his own. He was diagnosed with laryngomalacia, which affected his breathing and feeding, and then suffered terrifying seizures at six months old. Those days were some of the hardest of my life, but they taught me how strong I could be. Every experience I had up to that point—especially my time working in healthcare—gave me the tools I needed to advocate for my son.

By 2017, we were ready for a fresh start. Jonathan, Ethan, and I made the big move back to Sarasota as a family, and it felt like coming home. The beaches, the sunshine, and the support of family and friends made the transition so much easier. We partnered with my brother, Will, in a window-cleaning business, and we still run and operate it together to this day. This leap of faith taught us the highs and lows of entrepreneurship. It wasn't easy; there were major setbacks, but it certainly taught us quickly how to adapt to business, deal with stress, and take on leadership.

This included visa challenges and the uncertainty of 2020, but we kept going. It made us stronger and bonded our family even more. It was a very difficult time dealing with moving across the Atlantic, building a new life, the huge change in the business, and setting up Ethan's new healthcare system.

At that time, I would come up for air and take a quick breath, only to be pulled under again! It became rather comical at times. The old saying, "If I don't laugh, I will cry," resonated with me a lot. Looking back now, although it was an extremely difficult period, it taught me a great deal and made us all stronger, both individually and as a family.

Through it all, I found ways to keep laughing. When life threw chaos at us, I'd shrug and say, "It is what it is," or, "Use the struggle to your advantage." And somehow, we did. Ethan's health improved with time and treatment, and today, he's a thriving, healthy, brilliant nine-year-old boy who fills our lives with joy.

In 2022, a single Instagram message changed everything for me. After years of visa restrictions, I finally became a permanent resident, free to pursue my passions. That message introduced me to the world of travel advising, and something clicked. I threw myself into the industry, building The Jet Set Travel Group and helping families like mine plan their adventures. Seeing my clients discover the world—and mentoring others to start their businesses in the travel industry—has been one of the most rewarding parts of my journey.

Then, in 2023, it all came full circle! Remember Parsons College and the fashion marketing dream I had way back in 2008? Rosa Tierra, our online clothing business, was born. It all started with a catch-up chat with my lifelong friend Catalina, again over Instagram! I had met her years earlier when we were flatmates in the UK. During the chat, we decided to curate elegant and sustainable fashion pieces from Colombia and South America. We had always dreamed of working together in fashion, and we were finally doing it! Within months, we were featured in British *Vanity Fair*! It felt like everything had come full circle. We are now selling in the United States and worldwide. I love how life has its way of connecting the dots.

Looking back, I can see how every challenge and setback has prepared me for where I am now. I've learned that resilience isn't just about surviving; it's about thriving, even when the odds feel stacked against you. Sarasota has given me so much: a beautiful community, the unwavering support of my family, and lifelong friends. I am truly grateful every day for what Sarasota has provided me! It has offered me many opportunities I never imagined and a place to truly call home. Thank you!

In 2025, I'm building and growing the businesses, working on continual self-development, helping others build their dreams, mentoring others on how to build a team and run their own business in the travel world, growing Rosa Tierra and working on my newest venture: becoming a jet broker!

Becoming a jet broker is another exciting endeavor that aligns perfectly with my passion for travel and entrepreneurship. By facilitating the buying, selling, and trading of private jets, I envision creating a unique niche that blends all aspects of the luxury travel world.

I will cater to clients who prioritize luxury and style in all aspects of their lives. Ultimately, becoming a jet broker will enable me to combine my interests, delivering unparalleled service in the realms of aviation, travel, and fashion while fostering lasting relationships within these industries. I can do all of this, while coaching others to do the same.

As I approach my fourth decade, I feel more grateful than ever. Life isn't about avoiding the tough times; it's about learning from them and using those lessons to build something beautiful. If there's one thing I've learned, it's that failure only happens when you stop trying. So, here I am, still trying, still dreaming, and still using my humour along the way.

You will find me traveling the world with family and friends, enjoying the freedom and adventure of being able to work from anywhere, and helping others build their dreams.

I'm truly grateful every day for where this journey has taken me so far, and for all the incredible connections and friendships I have made along the way.

Cheers to the next chapters!

# From Chaos to Confidence: The Story of Jennifer Matteo Event Planning

Jennifer Matteo

Jennifer Matteo is a dynamic and accomplished entrepreneur known for her creativity, organizational expertise, and passion for creating unforgettable experiences. As the founder and lead designer of Jennifer Matteo Event Planning, she has become one of the most sought-after event planners in South Florida, as well as luxury locations worldwide.

Originally from a small town outside of Philadelphia, Jennifer's love for design and event production began early, inspiring her to pursue a career in events that seamlessly blend artistry with creativity. Since launching her business in 2015, she has curated a diverse portfolio of events, including luxury weddings, corporate functions, and philanthropic galas, all characterized by her signature style—bold, personalized, and meticulously crafted.

Jennifer's approach is deeply collaborative, tailoring each event to reflect her clients' unique personalities and stories. Her attention to detail and ability to transform visions into reality have earned her accolades from both clients and industry peers. She has been featured in top publications such as *The Knot*, *Style Me Pretty*, *Grace Ormond*, and more locally, *Sarasota Magazine*.

Beyond her professional success, Jennifer is an active member of her community, supporting local businesses and nonprofits through her work. When she's not designing stunning events, she enjoys spending time with her family, exploring Sarasota's vibrant arts scene, and staying inspired by the ever-evolving world of design.

Jennifer Matteo's passion for excellence and dedication to her craft continue to make her a leader in the event planning industry, creating memories that last a lifetime.

@JenniferMatteoEventPlanning

———

It all started with a meltdown. Picture this: I'm sitting in my car after work, mascara streaked down my cheeks, replaying the day in my head. My boss? An absolute dick. Every interaction felt like a power struggle, every email a test of patience. I was miserable, and for what? A paycheck that didn't even begin to justify the emotional toll. That day, I made the boldest—and maybe craziest—decision of my life: *I quit.*

Walking away from stability wasn't easy, but I had no idea that that leap of faith would become the foundation for Jennifer Matteo Event Planning (JMEP). I didn't have a roadmap, just a dream and a nagging feeling that I could do it better. But starting a business? Oh, honey. No one tells you it's not all Pinterest boards and champagne toasts. It's messy. It's chaotic. And it's absolutely worth it.

## Dining Room Hustle: Baby, Puppy, and Pure Chaos

Fast-forward a few weeks, and there I was: working from home, crammed into my dining room, a baby latched to my breast, and a puppy gleefully peeing in the corner. This was the glamorous life of an entrepreneur, right? Wrong. It was complete and utter chaos. I'd have a client consultation on Zoom while soothing a crying baby with one hand and frantically trying to clean up puppy accidents with the other. The vibe was less "boss babe" and more "help, I'm drowning."

But somehow, amidst the whirlwind of diapers, deadlines, and dog pee, I pulled off an entire wedding season, on my own. It wasn't pretty, but it worked. I remember sitting down after that first season and finally—finally—taking a breath. I had survived. More importantly, I had learned. And lesson number one? *Working from home is not for me—I gotta go.*

## The Office Era: Building JMEP's Foundation

With one season under my belt, I knew things had to change. The dining room hustle wasn't cutting it anymore. I needed a space—a real office where I could meet clients, collaborate with my newly growing team, and, you know, not trip over squeaky toys on my way to a meeting. Securing that office felt like a turning point. It was a physical representation of JMEP's growth, a sign that this dream was becoming a reality.

Our second season came in hot, and the numbers were staggering: over 100 events in a single year. Weddings, parties, corporate gatherings—you name it, we did it. Each event was its own mini-production, requiring creativity, precision, and a whole lot of caffeine. We were in the zone, firing on all cylinders. And then... *COVID*.

## Back to Square One: The COVID Reset

When the pandemic hit, it was like someone pressed a giant reset button on the entire world—and JMEP was no exception. Overnight, events were canceled, postponed, or scaled down to tiny backyard affairs. I went from juggling a packed calendar to staring at a very empty one. It was heartbreaking, watching all that momentum screech to a halt. And just like that, I was back to square one: alone, rebuilding from scratch.

But if there's one thing I've learned, it's that resilience isn't optional in this business. So, I rolled up my sleeves and got to work. It started with rebuilding my team. I handpicked individuals who shared my vision and passion, people who weren't just talented but also kind and collaborative. Together, we poured our energy into nurturing relationships—with clients, vendors, and the community. We knew that laying the groundwork during these quiet months would pay off when the world reopened.

## Relationships Are Everything: Clients and Vendors

In the event planning world, relationships are the secret sauce. During those rebuilding months, I focused heavily on creating strong connections with clients and vendors. I wanted JMEP to be synonymous with trust, creativity, and excellence. This meant long phone calls, socially distanced coffee dates, and plenty of Zoom meetings to reassure everyone that we were still here, still committed, and ready to deliver when the time came.

Vendors became allies in a way I hadn't anticipated. We shared leads, brainstormed ways to adapt, and supported one another through the uncertainty. That sense of community was a silver lining I'll always be grateful for. It reminded me that success isn't about doing it alone; it's about building something bigger together.

## Back in Full Swing: JMEP Today

As the world slowly found its footing again, so did JMEP. The phones started ringing, the inquiries rolled in, and our calendar filled up once more. But this time, we were stronger, smarter, and more intentional about how we operated. We weren't just surviving; we were thriving.

Today, JMEP handles over 100 events a year with the kind of confidence and finesse that comes from experience. We've seen it all—bridezillas, torrential rain on outdoor weddings, last-minute cancellations—and we've handled it with grace (and maybe a little wine afterward). Our team is a well-oiled machine, balancing creativity with logistics to make each event unforgettable.

## Lessons Learned: Chaos Is the Path to Greatness

Looking back, it's almost comical how chaotic those early days were. From the baby on my hip to the puppy in the corner, it felt like I was in over my head 24/7. But that chaos taught me resilience. It forced me to think on my feet, to adapt, and to trust my instincts. Every tear, every sleepless night, every moment of doubt led me here.

JMEP isn't just a business; it's a testament to perseverance, creativity, and a little bit of stubbornness. It's proof that starting messy doesn't mean you won't end up polished. And most importantly, it's a reminder that the best things in life come from taking risks, embracing the chaos, and never giving up—even when your dining room smells like puppy pee.

## The Future of JMEP

As I sit here today, reflecting on this wild journey, I can't help but feel excited for what's next. The events industry is ever-changing, and we're ready to evolve with it. Whether it's incorporating new trends, embracing sustainability, or finding innovative ways to wow our clients, JMEP is here for it.

But one thing will never change: our commitment to creating unforgettable experiences. From the first consultation to the final dance, every event we plan is crafted with care, creativity, and a whole lot of heart. And that, my friend, is the magic of Jennifer Matteo Event Planning.

Here's to the next chapter. Cheers!
With Glamour & Grace,
Jennifer

# My Journey from Silenced to Unstoppable

## Emily J. Meinke

Emily Meinke grew up in Mason, Mich., where she spent her childhood training and competing as an elite gymnast. She graduated from Michigan State University with a bachelor of science degree in psychology and worked in the financial industry for 15 years as a certified IRA services professional, marketing self-directed retirement accounts and non-traditional investment strategies. Emily lived and worked in Arizona and Texas before moving to Florida in 2015.

When her son was born in 2018, Emily left corporate life to focus on her family and simultaneously began her journey of entrepreneurship, exploring multiple business ventures. She also jumped into the world of advocacy when she disclosed childhood sexual abuse that spanned her entire gymnastics career and into adulthood at the hands of Larry Nassar, the USA Gymnastics team physician. As a result, Emily received the Foundation for Global Sports Development's Humanitarian Award and the Arthur Ashe Award for Courage at the ESPYs and was one of the honorees of *Glamour Magazine's* Women of the Year Award along with her fellow Sister Survivors. She is a passionate survivor advocate, speaking publicly about her experience to raise awareness and to educate people on how to recognize red flags, and works closely with legislators supporting widespread changes surrounding the prevention of sexual assault and working toward passing Survivor's Rights bills nationwide. Emily helped launch The Army of Survivors and currently serves on the board for the Junior League of Sarasota and on the auxiliary for SPARCC in Sarasota. She also volunteers with RISE.

https://www.instagram.com/emilyj.meinke
https://www.facebook.com/emily.j.meinke

———

**The Day My Voice Became My Power**

It was January 23, 2018. I caught an early flight from Florida, and upon landing, headed straight to the courthouse in Lansing, Mich. Sitting in the back of the courtroom, the air was heavy with stillness as I waited my turn. When my name was called, I felt my chest tighten. My knees were weak as I walked toward the front. I wasn't sure if I was ready, but I knew it was time. Time to face him and reclaim part of me he tried to steal. The eyes of every person in the room fell on me, yet I stared only at him. When I opened my mouth to speak, my words came not from the typed pages in front of me, but from somewhere deeper inside, they were carved into my soul.

For years I carried the weight of his actions on my own, but standing there with a hundred survivors' voices echoing in my mind, I felt something new: solidarity. The courage I found in that moment wasn't mine alone, it was built on the strength of others who had spoken before me. My voice didn't belong solely to the woman standing at the podium—it also belonged to the little girl inside me who had been silenced for so long. She was finally ready to be heard.

I spoke my truth, loud and clear, as it streamed live worldwide. My victim impact statement described vividly in detail the years of horrific abuse I suffered at the hands of Larry Nassar, the USA Gymnastics doctor, and it was then and there that everyone learned my deep, dark, secret. This is the day my purpose and path changed forever.

## The Silence Between the Stories

When I left the courthouse that afternoon, I experienced a new sense of freedom. I had just spoken my truth out loud for the very first time! Before then, not a soul knew—not my parents, my husband, my former teammates, or my friends. In some ways, I felt like the weight of the world was lifted that day; however, I quickly became aware of the heaviness of a truth far greater than my own.

As I walked past reporters eagerly waiting with microphones and cameras, and past the crowd of young gymnasts shivering in the cold outside the building holding posters showing support and offering encouragement, I couldn't help but think about my old teammates—the ones who had been through the same horror but weren't in the courtroom that day. Some couldn't come forward, still bound by fear or shame. Others chose not to, feeling the betrayal of a system that had already let them down too many times. Their silence wasn't a choice, it was survival. A method I completely understood and had lived for decades.

As I lay awake that night, their faces filled my mind as I replayed the voices of the brave women who told their stories in court, all eerily similar, filling the room like a symphony of resilience. Yet what haunted me most were the stories I hadn't heard—the ones trapped in silence, the ones that might never be told. My vision and purpose began to take shape and I knew this chapter of my life couldn't end here. I was being called to stand for all survivors, now and in the future—for a world where fewer people endure what we endured. I vowed to fight for survivors' rights, ensuring that every person who dared to come forward would be met with the support and justice they deserve.

Together with my sister survivors, we propelled the #MeToo movement into the spotlight in the months following sentencing, reigniting a global conversation about the prevalence of sexual violence and the strength of survivors. It swept across industries, nations, and generations, uniting us in our shared pain, and more importantly, our collective resilience. This movement wasn't just about speaking out; it was about keeping the conversation alive and making sure the world could no longer look away.

While the headlines eventually faded, my work had just begun. Advocacy became my mission. It isn't glamorous or easy, yet I could not stay silent. Advocacy means having difficult conversations, standing up to powerful institutions and systems that too often fail survivors, and pushing for change in a world that doesn't always want to hear its shortcomings.

Soon I began working with the Sarasota Safe Place and Rape Crisis Center (SPARCC), supporting survivors of domestic violence and sexual assault, along with their children who too often carry the weight of trauma in silence.

My advocacy extends to the halls of power. Through my work with RISE, I fight for survivors' rights legislation, pushing for laws that protect survivors in court and advocating for policies that improve access to justice.

I am carrying the torch as part of a greater movement fighting not just for justice, but for a world where the cycle of silence and abuse is broken.

## Unearthing All That Was Buried

Immediately following the sentencing, I felt a huge sense of relief. I had spoken my truth and reclaimed my voice. I also became acutely aware that the hardest part of the process was just beginning, and the difficult work would come when I took a hard look inward and started to pick up the pieces.

For decades, I compartmentalized my pain, packaging my emotions in a tightly sealed box, locking it away, inaccessible, in hopes it would one day be forgotten. I had to be strong, to keep moving forward, to prove to the world—and myself—that I was OK. As I stood front and center that day in court, the lid on that box cracked open and everything I had buried for decades began rising to the surface.

Overwhelming waves of grief came first and seemingly out of nowhere. Grief for the carefree little girl I never really got to be, the girl who can barely remember a time when the world appeared safe. Then came the anger—hot, fierce, and unapologetic. Anger at the man who had stolen my innocence. Anger at myself, misplaced perhaps, for staying silent and carrying shame and guilt that was never mine to bear. And most of all, anger at the people and institutions who failed to protect me and the hundreds, if not thousands, of survivors who suffered at the hands of Larry Nassar.

Possibly the most challenging sensation to work through was the profound emptiness within. See, gymnastics all but defined my past. Everyone in my hometown knew me as "the gymnast." In the courtroom, the pictures painted by the victims exposed the dark side of the elite gymnastics culture, strategically hidden behind the plethora of trophies and medals. The world got a glimpse behind the scenes at the ecosystem we navigated including coaches, doctors, and institutions who were hyper-focused on winning championships, and who played a monumental role in shaping our lives. The consistent message that came through loud and clear was that each of us was disposable and replaceable. Perfection was the standard and if you weren't up for it, get out of the way.

While I was aware of the immense pressure and demands that came with this caliber of competition, I had no clue its impact was so far-reaching and more detrimental than I could have ever imagined.

Perhaps this is why the notion of self-worth was non-existent for me as far back as I can remember. I didn't just *struggle* to love myself—I didn't *believe* I deserved love at all. There was a constant record playing in my head repeating "You aren't enough, you never were."

Through years of exploring different modalities such as therapy, leadership training, and energy work, I've learned that healing isn't about erasing the scars, it's about embracing and understanding them—letting go of the shame and learning to embrace the parts of myself I had long rejected. I learned that my value is not defined by how much I give or how much I achieve. I started by looking in the mirror and trying to see the person beneath the pain, and beyond the labels of "survivor" and "advocate." I began to ask myself, "What does it mean to love yourself, to feel worthy, just as you are?"

The answers didn't come easily, but slowly I began to realize my worth isn't tied to my past, my pain, or even my resilience. It simply existed.

## Learning to Honor Myself

For as long as I can recall, I believed that in order to "be strong" I must push through the pain, ignore warning signs, and persevere no matter what; a mindset cultivated within the culture of elite athletics. I had been conditioned to think that caring for myself was an act of indulgence, not a necessity.

Somewhere along my healing journey, I started to understand the truth that changed my perspective: until I took care of my own mental health, I couldn't care for others. I couldn't advocate, couldn't support those who needed me, and couldn't fight for the change I wanted to see in the world. I learned that honoring my mental health means allowing myself the grace to rest without guilt. It's OK to say no, without an explanation.

At first, it felt foreign. Every time I took a step back to breathe or took time for myself, I felt selfish and weak. Over time and with practice, it's becoming easier, although, many days, I still struggle. The guilt creeps back in, the self-doubt that I'm not doing enough, that *I'm not enough*. But now I recognize those feelings without letting them control me. I'm still learning to give myself the compassion that I so freely offer to others.

I recognize now that self-care is also about honoring my body. I've adopted a holistic approach to well-being, understanding that my health is interconnected. When my body feels good, my mind follows, and vice versa. I am intentional about nourishing my body with the same love and care that I'm learning to give my mind. I started focusing on proper nutrition, ensuring I'm fueling my body with what it needs to function at its best. I pay attention to what I put into my body, from fresh, wholesome foods to essential supplements that support my overall health. I only expose my body to non-toxic cleaning supplies, lotions, shampoos, makeup, and clothing free of forever chemicals.

I also learned to approach exercise in a way that's kind to my body—not pushing beyond my limits, but rather incorporating regular, restorative movement. Sometimes that means yoga or Pilates, a walk or run in the sunlight, or strength training. Incorporating safe detox methods like infrared sauna sessions and prioritizing mindful meditation to nourish my soul are also non-negotiables in my wellness routine.

There are days I can't shake the feeling I should be doing more, but now, I've reframed my thinking to trust that self-care is an act of strength, not weakness; it's about self-preservation, not indulgence. It's about staying well so I can continue this journey and do the work that matters.

## Building the Future Together

If anything, my work in advocacy has revealed clearly that sexual assault isn't just a series of isolated incidents; it's an epidemic. It seeps into every corner of society, hidden behind closed doors, whispered in hushed tones, and buried in silence. The statistics—one in three, one in four—don't accurately capture the scope of what I have seen, felt, and heard, as we know those numbers only represent cases that have been reported.

While I don't have all the answers, I know for sure that we can no longer allow survivors to feel like their stories don't matter, like their voices don't deserve to be heard. This is what fuels my belief that together we can create something powerful— something that will last beyond our lives, a legacy of strength, love, and support for generations to come, and that is what I intend to do. We are stronger together, and every step we take toward healing is a victory, no matter how small.

My story is not just mine alone—it's the story of every survivor who has ever felt silenced, invisible, or unworthy. We must continue to share our stories, to create spaces where we can heal, empower, and support one another, and in doing so, finally break the cycle of shame and give ourselves the gift of freedom. The journey continues, and with every voice, every story, every step forward, we are creating a world where survivors are no longer just surviving—but thriving.

As I stand sturdy on the path I've walked—through pain, silence, and courage, I am aware that healing isn't a destination, but a journey that never truly ends and doesn't come with a map or finish line. It's a journey of growth, self-discovery, and learning to embrace every part of our being. The process is anything but linear, but with each step, I'm discovering more about the person I was always meant to be and the gifts I was given to share with the world.

# Single AND Slaying

## Heather Palo

Heather Palo: Guided by Faith, Rooted in Community

Heather Palo is a Sarasota native whose life is shaped by her deep faith, strong community ties, and love for her coastal hometown. Born and raised in a city where sunshine, salty air, and the rhythm of the waves are a way of life, Heather cherishes Sarasota's natural beauty and vibrant culture.

A black belt in Taekwondo and a two-time Junior Olympic gold medalist, Heather pursued her Olympic dreams until two major back surgeries redirected her path. Despite this setback, her passion for martial arts remains, and she continues to share her love for the sport through coaching whenever she can.

As the CEO of Palo Premier Homes, Heather has established herself as a leading figure in Sarasota's luxury real estate market. Known for her dedication, expertise, and ability to connect families with their dream homes, she turns aspirations into reality while showcasing the unparalleled lifestyle Sarasota has to offer.

Heather's personal life is just as dynamic as her professional one. Whether she's paddleboarding across the Gulf, diving for shark teeth, or simply savoring the ocean's serenity, her connection to the sea is a constant source of inspiration. A lover of music and worship, she leads with grace at SRQ House Church, using her talent to uplift others and share her faith.

Family plays a central role in Heather's life, with her nephews holding a particularly special place in her heart. Her adventurous spirit has taken her across the globe, where she embraces diverse cultures and experiences that enrich her perspective and bring depth to her work and personal life.

Heather's story is one of resilience, passion, and purpose—a testament to her unwavering belief in the power of faith and community.

Follow her journey on social media: @realtorpalo.

———

Being single doesn't define me, nor does it dictate the woman I am becoming. It's not a limitation; it's simply a season, a chapter in my journey. This chapter in my life is one of discovery, growth, and understanding what it truly means to be chosen—not by the world, but by me and, most importantly, by God. And my journey, like all good stories, has been filled with unexpected heartache, crushed dreams, and perseverance.

I was born and raised in Sarasota, Fla., where the waves crashing on the shore and the salty air were more than just part of the scenery—they were part of my soul. This city, with all its beauty, has been my constant, even as life brought unexpected twists and turns. Sarasota is where my story began, and it's where I've learned to navigate life's challenges, anchored by my faith, surrounded by my incredible family, and driven by the love of my community.

I was raised by my beautiful, resilient, amazing mother—a force of nature, and my greatest supporter. Because of this, along with the unwavering love and support from my Gram, my childhood was full of laughter, adventure, and strength. My older brother, just 13 months older than me, was my best friend. We were inseparable. We spent many days running barefoot through the neighborhood, climbing trees, letting our imaginations create new worlds, and chasing our dreams until the sun dipped below the horizon.

I was a confident, carefree, and strong-willed little girl. I knew what I wanted and wasn't afraid to go after it. At one point, I was convinced I was going to be a Spice Girl—that or a figure skater like Michelle Kwan. I was always singing and dancing and pretending to skate in my living room or performing in my friend's garage. I was full of life, imagination, and the dream of marrying an NSYNC member. The only fear I had was of my father.

Unfortunately, childhood dreams don't shield you from life's realities. Not every childhood memory I have is joyful. Our father wasn't the kind of man you looked up to. He was manipulative, abusive, and absent in all the ways that mattered. I saw his darkness even as a child and tried to protect the people I loved from it. He had many wives and multiple children and although I am so grateful for all of my brothers and sisters, I wish so many people didn't have to suffer because of one broken person. The challenges all of us have endured have shaped us in ways that we are still unpacking.

I was nine years old when my world cracked wide open. My brother decided to move in with our father, who lived an hour and a half away; he promised my brother all the things my single mom couldn't afford. Our father had been expecting another son. He manipulated my brother into believing he was a burden to my mom and that he was doing her a favor by leaving. I wasn't surprised that I wasn't offered the same deal. He knew he couldn't manipulate me, and he knew I didn't like him. Plus, he didn't have anything to do with his other two daughters.

I remember the sadness in my mom's eyes and the heartbreak etched into her being. A pain so profound it burned into my memory. I'll never forget that day, how my brother's choice left my mom shattered and left me feeling abandoned. A piece of my mom was left behind that day. His physical absence left a hole in my life and in my heart that I didn't know how to fill.

I didn't know it then, but that moment changed me. After he left, I became quiet, insecure, and unsure of myself. I didn't know who I was without him. That confident little girl who once danced without fear and dreamed without limits seemed to disappear. I suddenly struggled to make friends, I no longer played, I gained weight and was bullied. I wasn't the only one who had changed, my brother had changed too. I knew he had to fight to survive in his new home, but on the very rare occasion I got to see him, we were no longer as close as we'd been before. Not only was I bullied by kids at school, but the bullying also came from my father and grandfather, and of course, my brother would chime in too. I was told I would never be as beautiful as that little girl in the tabloids whose name lived on after her tragic murder. My self-worth crumbled under the weight of cruel words, mocking, and abuse. I carried their words as scars shaping how I viewed myself. I longed for validation, for someone to tell me I was good enough just as I was. That longing shaped much of my young life. I spent years chasing an ideal of being beautiful enough, smart enough, and worthy enough for someone to stay, to choose me.

For years, I searched for that validation. I wanted to be seen, chosen, and loved—not just for who I could become, but for who I was. That need for acceptance shaped so much of my early life, leaving me vulnerable but also forging a strength I didn't yet understand.

At 14, the world of Taekwondo discovered me at a kickboxing class, and it felt like the beginning of a comeback. For the first time in years, I felt strong and was relearning who I was. My mom, ever my biggest cheerleader, worked two jobs to support me and my competing. I poured my heart and soul into Taekwondo, juggling straight A's in school with relentless training. I wasn't just good; I was exceptional. I earned my black belt, became a two-time Junior Olympic gold medalist, and rediscovered my confidence. On the mat, I felt invincible. Taekwondo wasn't just a sport for me; it was a way of life, my passion, my escape, and my proof that I could do anything I wanted.

My dream was to make it to the Olympics. By the age of 20, my body began to betray me. Herniated discs that were cracked and pushing against my nerves left me in excruciating pain, robbing me of my ability to walk without agony. The wear and tear of training had caught up with me, and I faced the harsh reality that my Olympic dream was no longer within reach. Two back surgeries later, I was left wondering who I was without the sport that had defined me. I lost a part of me and the strength and confidence I'd fought so hard to reclaim felt stripped away once more.

And just when I thought the challenges couldn't stack any higher, the doctors found lumps on my thyroid that were growing at a rapid pace. They were unsure if they were cancerous, and I underwent a partial thyroidectomy. The uncertainty was terrifying. I was told that my voice—the part of me that connected with my faith and brought me peace—might never be the same.

Yet even in the darkest moments, God showed His grace. The thyroid nodules were benign, and though the journey after surgery has not been easy, I persevered, and every note I sing is a testament to resilience and faith.

Against all odds, I was able to return to Taekwondo after my surgeries. Through perseverance, faith, and sheer determination, I reclaimed my place on the mat. Not only did I compete again, but I went on to win multiple gold medals, proving to myself that setbacks don't define us—our comebacks do.

Life, in its beautiful unpredictability, has brought healing and unexpected blessings. My brother found his way home and our bond was restored as if it never left. My mom has her son back and gained a daughter-in-law. I'm forever grateful to his wife for helping him get out of that insufferable situation and for being the sister and friend I never knew I needed. Today, we live right down the street from one another, and they have brought such a gift to our family. My nephews, the tiny humans I never knew I could love so deeply, expanded my heart in ways I never imagined, reminding me that God's blessings often come in unexpected forms.

I never understood God's plan for taking my brother away from our home, but I now understand that he needed to be in that house for our younger brother, who is finally out as well, and lives close to us with his wife—my other amazing sister and friend.

Faith became the foundation of my journey. In 2016, I was baptized, and one by one, my family followed. Watching my mom, my brothers, and their wives come to Christ has been my greatest answered prayer.

God may not have brought a husband or children into my life yet, but He has given me something far greater: a family united in faith and love.

I'll admit, there are many days when I dream of getting married and having children of my own. Maybe that's in God's plan for me, and maybe it's not. What I do know is that I no longer wait for someone else to define my life. I have already overcome and accomplished many things as a single woman.

Today, I am living a life that I love. As a successful realtor, I get to help families find their dream homes, creating spaces where their own stories can unfold. My work isn't just about houses—it's about building lives, fostering connections, and being a part of people's most cherished moments. I have built a business that allows me to travel, exploring the world and soaking in its beauty and diversity. I lead worship at SRQ House Church, sharing my voice and my faith with a community that so quickly felt like home. I get to spend time with my family, creating memories that I will cherish forever, and I get to be an aunt who is present and so involved in my nephews' growth and well-being.

Through it all, my mom has been my rock. She's the first person I call in moments of joy or need, the woman who has always answered the phone and rescued me, no matter the hour. Her strength, love, and untiring support have shaped me into the woman I am today. She taught me what it means to persevere, to love without conditions, and to never give up.

It took me 35 years to realize that I had been sitting on the sidelines of my own life, waiting. Waiting to be chosen, waiting to live up to society's standards, waiting for someone to tell me my time hasn't run out. For so long, I thought my life would only begin when someone chose me—when a man looked at me and decided I was "the one." I was exhausted from hearing about my "ticking clock" as if my worth was tied to having a husband and children. Here's the truth: my value isn't defined by someone else's timeline or expectations.

What I've learned is that life isn't about waiting to be chosen—it's about choosing yourself.

Being single isn't a limitation, it's an opportunity. It's a season to grow, to discover who I am, and to embrace the life that God has given me. I wake up every day and choose to live boldly, say "yes" to adventure, love deeply, and celebrate the wins and the blessings in my life. I don't know how my story will end, or whether marriage and children are in God's plan for me, but I do know that I am exactly where I am meant to be.

The Bible says we are a chosen people, a royal priesthood. He has already chosen us. He has chosen us for this very moment in history, so what will you do with it?

So, here I am, single and slaying, living a life that's mine. My story isn't finished yet, but I know it is being written with purpose, resilience, and love.

To the little girl I once was, who thought she lost herself in the battle: You will always find your way. You will rise up, time and time again, because that's who you are. You are a child of God, a daughter of a King. You are beautiful, loved, enough, and always chosen by Him.

# The Power of Creative

# Imagination

## Jessica Papineau

Jessica Papineau, the founder of CSJ, a leading styling company for high-performing female entrepreneurs—and other women who simply want to look and feel their best—has spent over 25 years in the fashion industry teaching women how to use fashion to serve their purpose, boost their confidence, and elevate their image. Jessica has styled thousands of women, from moms struggling to dress their postpartum bodies, to business women seeking to level up their careers, to seven-figure entrepreneurs, and professionals in the entertainment, sports, and music industries. With a goal of helping women imagine more for themselves, break free from what's holding them back, and show the world who they truly are, Jessica is committed to empowering women to elevate their style and transform their careers, relationships, and lives.

Instagram: @thejessicapapineau
Facebook: Customized Styling by Jessica
LinkedIn: Jessica Papineau
Youtube: Customized Styling by Jessica

———

If you looked at me now—a woman deeply passionate about helping women feel beautiful and step into their power through fashion—you might never guess how it all began. My story didn't start in brightly lit boutique dressing rooms or on stages speaking to hundreds of women about owning their confidence. It started in the backwoods of Maine, in a small cabin without electricity, a phone, or even running water.

I was an only child until the age of eight, when my mom married my stepdad, and I gained two sisters. They spent every summer and school vacation with us, and when I was 11, my mom and stepdad had a child together, giving me another sister. I was raised by my mother and stepfather, who chose to live off the land. Our meals were grown in our garden, and our winters were warmed by a single wood-burning stove. We had kerosene lanterns to light our home at night, a well and hand pump as our water source, and an outhouse. Life was simple, but not easy. I remember standing in that little house, looking out at the thick woods that surrounded us, and wondering why I had been placed there. Why was I born into a family that didn't share my love for beauty and style? Why did I feel so different, and like I was meant for something else?

The lack of modern conveniences wasn't the hardest part; it was the loneliness. Without electricity, there was no TV to occupy my time, no phone to call friends, and the only entertainment I had was what I could create for myself. My love for fashion began out of necessity. My clothes came from the Salvation Army, but to me, they were magical. I would try them on in front of a full-length mirror, pairing pieces in creative ways, and pretend I was at elegant parties having the time of my life surrounded by people who valued me, and loved being in my presence. For those moments, I didn't feel like the awkward girl from the woods—I felt beautiful, confident, and powerful.

I didn't have much, but I had my imagination. And that, I've come to realize, was my superpower.

## Discovering My Gift

When I was 16, I moved to Winnipeg, Manitoba to live with my dad and grandmother. For the first time, I felt a spark of possibility. This was my chance to leave the woods behind and step into the world I'd always dreamed of. I remember stepping off the plane, looking at the city skyline, and feeling like my life was about to change for the better.

The first thing I did was put on my best outfit—a black skirt suit, nylons, and pumps—and head to the largest mall in the city. After getting off the city bus, with my resume, typed on an old typewriter, I walked from store to store, nervously handing it out. By the end of the day, my feet ached, and I was ready to give up. But I decided to try one more store—a women's clothing shop tucked away in a quiet corner of the mall.

The manager looked at my resume—completely void of retail experience—and decided to take a chance on me. I couldn't believe it; I was finally going to work in fashion.

But my excitement quickly faded when I realized the store catered to plus-sized women. As a tall, lanky teenager, I couldn't understand why these women didn't want my help. They avoided my suggestions, ignored my greetings, and, most painfully, waved me off with a dismissive hand.

It wasn't until a month into the job that something shifted. A woman named Kathy came in, desperate for an outfit that would make her feel confident at an upcoming conference. Like so many before her, she was skeptical of my help. But when she tried on the pieces I'd selected for her and saw herself fully styled in the mirror, something magical happened. Tears filled her eyes as she looked at me and said, "For the first time in my life, I feel beautiful."

That moment changed everything. I realized that fashion wasn't just about clothes; it was about transformation. It was about helping women see themselves in a way they never had before.

## The Leap of Faith

Years later, after marrying my soulmate and having two beautiful boys, I found myself in Sarasota, Florida, managing a high-end boutique. I had worked my way up, turning my passion into a career. I loved helping women discover their beauty by creating outfits for them that made them feel amazing, but I couldn't shake the feeling that I was meant for more.

My husband, a constant source of encouragement, always believed in me, even when I doubted myself. "You have a gift, Jess," he would say. "You were born to help women transform their lives."

One morning, on my drive to work, I was listening to a Tony Robbins podcast. He said something that stopped me in my tracks: "If you have a gift that can make a massive positive impact on others, it's selfish not to share it." Those words hit me like a lightning bolt.

In that moment, I realized that my fear of stepping out on my own wasn't protecting me; it was holding me back. I made the decision then and there to lean into my faith and trust that I was being guided toward something greater.

The transition wasn't easy. I had no roadmap, no safety net, just a belief that I was capable of something more, and a desire to show my two sons that they could do anything they put their minds to. My husband was my rock during this time, reminding me to take it one step at a time, and that no matter what I always had a soft place to land at home with my family. I started small, going to clients' homes to curate their wardrobes. I would mix their existing pieces with new ones I brought from local boutiques, creating looks that aligned with their lifestyle and aspirations. Slowly but surely, my side hustle grew.

## Moments of Transformation

One of my most memorable clients was a woman named Jennifer. Jennifer was a mom and a successful high-level executive at a financial firm who had recently gone through a divorce. When I arrived at her home, she confessed that she felt lost. She told me that she would get up every morning and put on clothing that she deemed "just good enough." "I don't even know who I am anymore," she said.

I first spent time getting to know more about Jennifer and about the life she truly desired for herself. She described what it would feel like to get the position of VP of sales and how she wanted to find true love and create a beautiful loving family for her children. I held the space with her as I imagined what she looked like as this woman she longed to be. I spent hours helping her let go of the pieces from her wardrobe that no longer served her, and replaced them with outfits that reflected the strong, independent woman she was about to become. When she looked in the mirror wearing a tailored blazer and sleek trousers, she smiled—a real, genuine smile. "I never knew that it was possible to look like and feel like this. For the first time I actually feel pretty, even beautiful," she said.

Stories like Jennifer's became the foundation of my work. I saw over and over how much a woman's outward appearance could impact her inner world. Clients who once felt invisible began to stand taller, speak louder, and pursue goals they had previously been too afraid to chase. As a result, these women were quickly closing the gap between where they were in their lives and where they desired to be. They were feeling more beautiful and confident. Their personal relationships were deepening, and they were getting job promotions and creating more successful businesses.

## The Lesson I Had to Unlearn

Growing up, I believed that my love for fashion and beauty was superficial. I thought it made me vain, shallow, or less worthy. But through my work, I've come to see the incredible transformation that happens when a woman feels beautiful. It's not about vanity; it's about empowerment.

When a woman looks in the mirror and loves what she sees, she shows up differently in the world. She speaks with confidence, walks with purpose, and shares her unique gifts with those around her. Fashion is just the vehicle—it's the tool that helps her step into her full power.

This realization didn't happen overnight. It took years of working with thousands of clients, witnessing their transformations, refining my craft and reflecting on my own journey to fully understand the depth of my work and the impact I was making in the world.

## The Heart of CSJ Styling

Today, CSJ Styling is so much more than a wardrobe service—it's a movement rooted in transformation. It's a space where women are seen, celebrated, and empowered to align their outward appearance with their inner brilliance.

CSJ Styling offers a range of services, from personalized styling sessions to our *Simplify and Elevate: The Wardrobe Edit*

*Digital Course.* At the heart of our offerings is the CSJ Styling Boutique Studio, featuring curated lines that perfectly align with our clients' unique lifestyles. We've developed an innovative app that connects women to styling tips, live events, digital courses, and a vibrant community of like-minded individuals. Whether it's creating a virtual lookbook tailored to a client's lifestyle or hosting a live Q&A session to answer pressing style questions, every interaction is designed to help women show up as the best versions of themselves.

The transformations I've witnessed through CSJ Styling have been nothing short of remarkable. Clients like Jennifer, a high-level executive recovering from a divorce, remind me why I started this journey. When she looked in the mirror wearing a tailored blazer and sleek trousers, she smiled—a real, genuine smile—and said, "I never knew it was possible to feel this way. For the first time, I feel beautiful."

These moments are the heartbeat of CSJ Styling. It's not just about the clothes; it's about helping women reclaim their confidence and step into the life they've always dreamed of.

## Looking Back, Moving Forward

When I reflect on my journey—from the backwoods of Maine to building a business that empowers women—I see how every step prepared me for where I am now. The isolation of my childhood taught me creativity and resilience. My early struggles in retail showed me the power of connection and empathy. And my husband's unwavering support reminded me that I was never alone in this journey.

Today, I feel an overwhelming sense of gratitude. For the clients who trust me to guide them. For the moments of transformation I've been privileged to witness. And for the little girl in the backwoods of Maine who, despite her doubts, dared to dream of a life bigger than the one she knew.

If there's one thing I've learned, it's this: No matter how small or insignificant your beginnings may feel, you are capable of extraordinary things. All it takes is a little faith, a lot of imagination, and the courage to lean into the possibilities waiting just beyond your comfort zone.

Because when you show up as someone who is meant to be seen, the world has no choice but to take notice. And that is the true power of transformation.

# The WOW Giving Blueprint:

# Designing a Life of Purpose and

# Impact

### Jessica Peterson

Jessica is an award-winning ICON real estate agent and coach with a dynamic background in banking, mortgages, and insurance. Known for her strategic mindset, she holds numerous certifications in real estate, business, charitable real estate, and life coaching. Her passion for planning began early—Jessica's dolls had carefully mapped-out lives with careers, finances, and volunteer commitments. In high school, she exemplified her belief in equality by resigning as homecoming princess, affirming that no one is better than anyone else.

Voted Best of SRQ in real estate and honored with international women's awards, Jessica is a best-selling author, TEDx speaker, and a community favorite in the real estate world. A life-changing experience when her husband was in ICU fueled her dedication to educating others about real estate and helping them design their ideal lifestyles with her proprietary systems.

Happily married for over 27 years, Jessica is a proud mother to a daughter who reminds her daily that miracles happen, defying the odds after being told she could never have children. A nature lover and advocate for intentional living, Jessica blends her professional success with heartfelt purpose. Her mission is to WOW one person daily and serve as the best wife, mother, and servant of God. Empowering others to achieve their dreams, Jessica's life is a testament to the power of perseverance, equality, and purpose-driven living.

https://www.facebook.com/jessicapetersonofficial
https://www.linkedin.com/in/jessicapetersonofficial/
https://www.instagram.com/jessicapetersonofficial/

———

"There is more happiness in giving than in receiving." — Acts 20:35

Scientific research has shown that giving not only benefits the recipient but also profoundly impacts the giver's well-being. Studies have revealed that acts of giving activate regions in the brain associated with pleasure, trust, and social connection, releasing endorphins and creating what some call a "helper's high." People who regularly give their time, resources, or support report higher levels of happiness and life satisfaction. Moreover, giving has been linked to improved physical health, including lower blood pressure and reduced stress levels. By understanding these benefits, we can appreciate that giving is a powerful tool not just for changing the world around us but for nurturing our own sense of purpose and well-being.

There's an extraordinary power in giving—one that transcends the act itself and ripples outward, impacting lives in ways we may never fully realize. Giving is about much more than simply sharing our resources; it's about choosing connection, empathy, and purpose. In this chapter, I'll take you through the deep-seated impact of giving, not just in the financial sense but in ways that touch people emotionally and spiritually.

My dream is to create a program called WOW Power Players; we are each on a mission to wow one person a day. Can you imagine hearing someone daily say *wow*? And the good that will come of it?

## The Power of Intention in Giving

The joy of giving is a unique kind of happiness that enriches both the giver and the recipient. But what truly elevates the experience of giving is the intention behind it. Intentional giving—when we give with thoughtfulness and purpose—turns a simple act into something powerful and lasting.

Often people say or think they want to give and then that thought disappears. Being intentional allows that thought to start and turn to action.

When we give with purpose, we're not just fulfilling a need or an obligation; we're acting from a place of empathy and connection. Our focus shifts from "What can I spare?" to "How can I serve?" By aligning our actions with our values and compassion, we create moments of giving that are meaningful and memorable. This focus allows even the smallest act to become a profound expression of care and connection.

## The Many Faces of Giving

Giving takes many forms. While financial support is often what we associate with philanthropy, true giving can come from our time, our knowledge, our compassion, and our energy. Giving might mean investing in someone's potential, volunteering time for a cause, listening deeply to someone who feels unheard, or guiding someone through challenges. The point is that giving is not limited to what we have but to who we are and what we choose to share.

### 1. Giving of Time

One of the most valuable things we can offer is our time. In a world filled with constant distractions and busy schedules, giving time means saying, "I value you enough to pause everything else." It might mean mentoring a young professional, volunteering at a shelter, or simply being present for a friend. Time is something we can never get back, making it one of the most genuine gifts.

### 2. Giving of Knowledge

Each of us carries unique knowledge and skills, hard-earned through experience. Sharing this knowledge allows us to create a ripple effect that extends beyond ourselves. When we teach, we empower others to grow, make better decisions, and elevate their lives. Imagine a world where everyone freely shared what they knew—the collective intelligence and kindness of humanity would reach unimaginable heights.

### 3. Giving of Spirit

Sometimes, the best thing we can give is our compassion. Being open-hearted and generous in spirit means we offer others our understanding, empathy, and support. It's about letting people know they're not alone in whatever they're facing. This form of giving reminds others of their intrinsic worth and fosters a connection that brings comfort and healing.

## Seeking Out Opportunities to Give

The opportunities to give are all around us, waiting for us to notice them. It's easy to think that giving requires a grand gesture or substantial resources, but often, the most meaningful acts of kindness are small and within reach. Developing a mindset that actively looks for ways to share kindness, time, or resources allows us to make a difference in everyday moments.

Every day, we encounter chances to lift others. A genuine compliment, a listening ear, or helping a colleague can make someone feel seen and valued. These small acts create a ripple effect, spreading positivity and support in ways we might never anticipate. Even a few minutes of undivided attention can mean the world to someone in a busy, often impersonal world.

To recognize these opportunities, start by looking around you. Is there someone in your life who could use a helping hand, or perhaps an organization that aligns with your passions? Often, the most impactful gifts are those that draw on our own experiences and strengths. When we give from a place of authenticity, we offer something truly valuable—a piece of ourselves.

What if those opportunities are not obvious? Start with asking people questions like, *what is a good connection for you?* Or, *what can I do to support you?* You will start to learn more about what a person needs or wants in life.

## Overcoming Obstacles to Giving

Many people hold back from giving, thinking they don't have "enough" to offer. It's a mindset that leads us to focus on scarcity rather than abundance. Here are some ways to overcome these barriers:

### 1. Redefine What You Have to Offer

Instead of focusing on financial constraints, recognize your non-monetary gifts. Time, kindness, and knowledge are things most of us can give in abundance. When we shift our mindset to understand that giving is not solely about money, we open ourselves up to new ways to contribute.

### 2. Find Purpose in Small Acts

Sometimes, we underestimate the impact of small gestures. A smile, a note of encouragement, or an act of kindness might seem minor, but they can be incredibly powerful. Realize that you don't have to make grand gestures to make a difference. Small acts, when done with sincerity, create meaningful change.

### 3. Balance

Understand how much time or money you can realistically give without jeopardizing your well-being, relationships, or financial stability. Focus on what you can and want to give. Often many opportunities come in our lives. It can be difficult to say *no*. Being focused on what you choose to give will help you to say *no* to things that may take you off track or off balance. It is OK to say *no*. How does one go about saying *no*? Here's a suggestion: "I won't be able to at this time. I'm currently focused on other projects and ways to give. Thank you for considering me; it means a lot."

### 4. Impact

Sometimes we want to make a large impact and realize we are unable to do it alone. Reach out to people who align with your values and want to join you on a larger mission.

## A Life of Generosity

To live a life of giving, we must cultivate generosity in small, everyday choices. Here are some simple ways to build this mindset:

### 1. Practice Gratitude
Regularly take note of what you have and what you can give, no matter how small.

### 2. Give Without Expectation
True giving means not expecting anything in return. This purity of intention is what makes giving meaningful and impactful.

### 3. Teach Generosity
If you have children, teach them the importance of giving. Lead by example, showing them that the greatest joy often comes from sharing what we have.

### 4. Say *Thank You*
If you notice someone is giving of their time or resources please tell them *thank you*. It can mean a lot!

### 5. Be Discreet
Not all acts of giving should be declared or known.

## Leaving a Legacy of Giving
Imagine what the world would be like if each of us were remembered not for what we achieved but for what we gave. Giving is one of the most profound ways to leave a legacy. It doesn't matter if the act is big or small—what matters is that it leaves a positive imprint on someone's life.

In your professional and personal life, strive to make giving a core value. Remember that giving is not only about others; it transforms us as well. Through giving, we learn empathy, we foster connections, and we find a purpose that reaches beyond ourselves.

If you strive to make a difference big or small and hear *wow* daily, please reach out to me. I would love to discuss ways to possibly work together.

# Here to Slay

## Courtney Petrin

Courtney Petrin is an award-winning interior designer who has been featured in *Architectural Digest*, *Vanity Fair*, and *Bon Appetit*, in addition to numerous local publications. She has been voted one of best interior designers by *SRQ Magazine* and Sarasota readers two years in a row. She has been voted one of the 100 Women to KNOW in Florida. She has been selected as a "Women on the Scene," a prestigious honor recognizing local women at the top of their game, as well as contributors to Sarasota.

In addition to these achievements, she was selected to be featured in *Sarasota Magazine's* Female Fortitude edition and voted as an honoree of Women Who Roar. She has been featured in *Tampa Voyage Magazine* and *She Exist Magazine*. Courtney has been interviewed and featured on SNN news twice. She has been interviewed on numerous podcasts where she has shared her experiences and knowledge as a self-made entrepreneur. Courtney holds a master's degree in clinical psychology and applies it endlessly to the design field and working with clients. She enjoys supporting other women and female-owned small businesses. Courtney enjoys doing random acts of kindness and has worked for numerous nonprofit organizations and volunteered at several mental health centers. She loves mentoring other aspiring designers and female entrepreneurs.

She is a mother and wife who values family above all else. She loves living in Sarasota and is thankful to the community that has allowed her to grow her business with her family.

https://www.instagram.com/savannahs_home_and_design

––––

When I think of the word *slay* the word *warrior* comes to mind—as in, someone who is ready for battle, and so dedicated to a cause that they are willing to die for it. *Business owner*, entrepreneur, and warrior: You might not think these words belong together, but to me, they are the same.

I remember it like it was yesterday.

I was getting ready for what would be our biggest project reveal to date. We had worked so hard on this project for the last year and a half, and I was so nervous. I was also elated because I knew in my heart our clients would love their home.

That day, I had just received an email from *Architectural Digest* on a potential feature opportunity. I was in total shock. I was on cloud nine and felt like I was in a daze. Things felt like they were finally clicking. I was immediately grounded by a message I received from someone on Facebook I didn't recognize. They didn't have a profile photo and I didn't recognize the name. I opened the message. When I started reading the first few words I immediately knew who it was from.

I could tell by the language and tone instantly. I felt, well...numb. I thought it was ironic that at the moments I can celebrate my small wins I'm reminded that in this person's mind, I'm still a child to them. They did the best they could with what they were given. I wasn't angry, mad, or bitter. I felt the irony of my life—my past and my history—at that moment. This part of my life and childhood that I'd tried so hard to escape reminded me how I can feel so small, even today. Our traumas always influence us, no matter how far away from them we get.

I think it's important to say that this is so often the life of an entrepreneur and anyone who has had to start at the bottom. I feel as though the concept of "success" is subjective and defined by how we measure it. I do feel I have lived my life authentically. I have been brave and fearless in my pursuit of my own happiness. I have made brave choices, changed my circumstances, and written my own destiny. This life wasn't given to me, and I was not afforded any advantages. I wasn't born on third base, and every huddle I jumped over, I earned. I created it, and I continue to cultivate it. I have poured into myself what I didn't get as a child, and in ways, I've parented myself. I still do. I think when you grow up understanding what your perceived worth is, you learn you need to define yourself and not allow others to do it for you.

It was no mystery to me that my life would lead to a career in psychology. I grew up with a front-row seat to adult challenges, and in many ways, psychology became my way of understanding some injustices I felt I witnessed or experienced. I spent eight years getting a master's degree in clinical psychology and rising through the ranks of positions within my field. Every goal I set for myself I exceeded—often at the expense of my own happiness and mental health. I pushed myself hard and achieved everything I planned to.

Yet, at the age of 28, I somehow had this nagging feeling I couldn't shake. I was no longer chasing a goal post, and this equilibrium allowed me to truly sit and examine my life. Something was missing. And I was conflicted by this feeling, even guilty for it. I had wanted all this, yet somehow it felt depressing.

Years spent watching HGTV with my husband Carlin and dabbling in our own home renovations kept me busy. We dreamed of moving south and flipping homes together. My husband, who was in the trades, had a natural love for anything to do with home building and renos, and I loved design. I also had no idea I was meant to be an entrepreneur. I didn't know what that meant at the time. I had no clue that I was not meant to work for someone else and that maybe that was a good thing. I didn't understand my own emotions, even though (ironically) I was making a living figuring out emotions. It was beyond frustrating, and as much as I tried to bury my feelings, they were always there. It wasn't until November of 2017 that it was as if the universe said, "We hear you, and here's your answer." I learned that, at 30 years old, I was four weeks pregnant.

Although we had tried earlier and I experienced a miscarriage, I was at peace with the fact that I may not be a mother. In fact, I didn't even have a strong connection to motherhood. I felt it was time and an appropriate step in life, but the call to be a mother had never been strong for me; I was a career-oriented person, and had been since I was 18 years old.

After learning I was pregnant, I think I spent the first week in total denial and shock. I was the planner of my life and I had the timing of everything down to the minute. I had no control over this. My shock was quickly followed by weeks and months of joy; after the nausea and sickness faded, I loved being pregnant. They say that a woman's brain changes during pregnancy, and I believe it wholeheartedly. For the first time in my life, I had complete clarity. I knew this life was no longer serving me. Living through winters and working in this field—the stress of which I had no say or control over—had totally burnt me out. I had no outlet for creative expression and I was tired, simply tired.

During my pregnancy, Carlin and I decided to make good on the dream we had had since we were 16 years old. At seven months pregnant, we put our house on the market and prepared for what would be the biggest change of our lives. The challenge of becoming first-time parents, moving your whole life, and changing careers all at once isn't one I'd recommend; It's enough to endure one major life change, but to do four simultaneously is insanity.

We moved to Florida and lived in our travel trailer for six weeks while we started our business. We then established our LLC and began the process of building connections. I cannot fully express the mental and marital strain of living in a travel trailer with a newborn and three dogs. To add to that, our only income was from the profit on the sale of our home in Massachusetts. That was our lifeline to our rental house, to live, and to secure our first investment property. We did feel some sense of relief once we moved into our rental home, but it was quickly followed by the pressure of our first flip and rehabbing it. Simply securing an investment property was a task. It was a lot of work, with endless sales falling through. Every deal lost meant another day without the promise of any future income.

We decided to bring in an investor to alleviate some of the financial burden on the flip we were funding. Once we completed and sold our first home here, we had some experience in the market in this area.

Our second one was equally stressful, and with this home we did 100 percent of the actual labor. My husband worked so hard on that home. I designed the home while I stayed home with our daughter. The financial strain was ongoing. When you are living off savings and there is no stream of steady income, it's extremely scary. Every day that we were not done with our flip was like watching our money being burned. It often felt dire.

This home did turn a better profit than the last one, but we still made out with pennies in the end. After paying the investor, his interest fees and closing fees, we were left with very little. But it wasn't all in vain. Our second home got some notice around town. It ended up being shared on quite a few social media platforms, and people were intrigued. We started getting inquiries from potential clients to design their homes. It wasn't a predetermined path at all. What began as a dream to be property investors and home rehabbers turned into a design and remodeling business. Although we received some really positive attention from our flips, we still needed to establish trust in the community. We spent two or three years simply doing that. We took any and every job, learned a ton, and built a reputation. All of our work came from word of mouth.

I had some truly amazing clients who took a chance on me in the early days, and I am immensely thankful to them. Today, I'm busier than ever, and I can choose the projects we take on. It was a hard road and challenging to get here. I feel privileged to live in paradise, raise our daughter here and run a business. The daily challenge of being a business owner keeps me humble. I feel I have so much more to personally accomplish, and it's important to know that life and a career is a path. It's not a goal post, a checkpoint, or a race to be run. It's full of turmoil, success, sadness, loss, and failure. The highs and lows are not lost on anyone.

Keep persevering, keep fighting for your dream, stay in the ring, and tune down the noise and negativity. The only way to truly slay is to be a warrior steadfast in her dream, despite hardship, and be willing to lay on the sword for it if it came to it.

# Learning to Say No in My Season

# of Yes

## Jerusha Pfannenschmidt

Jerusha Pfannenschmidt is a professional photographer offering a luxury photography experience like no other, and she runs a nonprofit with her boyfriend called Bettering Beaches. She is also a beach volleyball player and coach and is all about faith, freedom, and fitness!

www.instagram.com/pfanntasticphotography
https://www.facebook.com/share/15X5fBuWMX/?mibext
id=qi2Omg
www.pfanntasticphoto.com

———

When I moved to Florida (the last free country), I was leaving Louisville, Ky., at the tail end of the pandemic. My business had suffered like many others due to shutdowns that lasted much longer than necessary. I was also going through a divorce, at the end of my 14-year marriage. I made the decision to take a leap of faith and follow a longtime dream the moment I saw a particular quote on Pinterest. In the brightest wake-up call kind of colors, the message hit me loud and clear: "If not now, then when?"

It's funny how we can go along on a path somewhat aimlessly for years on end, knowing that there's a better life on the other side of indecision.

I've known all my life that New Albany, Ind., where I was born and raised, wasn't my forever home and felt the same way for the 15 years I lived in Louisville. Of course, my family and friends were home to me, but not the place. Growing up in a middle-class fam—nah, I'm not going there. Though I will say we were a family of eight on one income. We didn't have much, but my parents did what they could to make sure we had a family vacation to the beach nearly every year. It was the thing we looked forward to all year long.

One year that stands out in my memory was the year our two-toned brown (yes brown) Ford van overheated the whole way, and we had to make more stops than I care to recall, spraying the radiator down and letting it rest before the next attempt. Every visit to a new beach town was exciting, and full of memories with my family that I will always cherish. You know how when you're driving to a destination you're excited about, you're so amped? As a kid, there's the "Are we there yet?"

question that gets asked a million times. When your vacation ends, the drive back is nowhere near as exciting. I remember always loving the visits, but when it was time to go back, that was that.

The first time I visited Sarasota was an entirely different experience. I was finally home! I knew it immediately. And now when I visit my family and friends back in Indiana and Kentucky, I am every bit as excited going to visit them as I am to return to my forever home in Sarasota. It's such a cool feeling to know you are exactly where you are meant to be!

Moving here was no small feat. I had burned through most of my savings because of work being so scarce, only had $1,200 in the bank, and was going through a divorce, as I mentioned. I knew no one in Sarasota. I knew where I wanted to be but had no idea how to accomplish it. I remember sitting down with God and having a very real conversation with Him. I said:

*God, I know the realities of this world, I know how expensive it is where I want to live, and I also know it's a new state and city. I know I have very little money to work with. Most importantly, I know whose I am. I know as your daughter that the rules of this world don't necessarily apply to me. I know that if this is where you want me to be you will make a way where there seems to be no way. I would love a three-bedroom two-bathroom place within 15 minutes of Siesta Key, at a price I can afford. Please help me to figure this out!*

That prayer led me to make a Craigslist ad—here's what it said:

*Hi, my name is Jerusha. I'm in the process of relocating to Sarasota from Louisville. I am going through a divorce and trying to get my house sold here. Ideally, I am looking to rent a room for six months to a year while I build my photography client base. I hope to find an older woman who could benefit from having a helping hand around the house, I'm a fantastic cook, very clean. I do have three cats, so hopefully I can find a home that would welcome my well-behaved babies.*

After over 100 very indecent responses, I was feeling quite discouraged. However, I finally got a response that made it all worthwhile. There was a lady in a rut of her own, looking to get into a better situation. We got on a call to see if we could get along. I had also found a private investor through the same ad, who after a few talks was willing to lend me the money to buy a place.

One thing led to another, and over Valentine's Day 2021, I boarded a plane to look at some places in Sarasota. Little did I know, everything would seem to fall apart on that trip. My plan was to try to move by the end of March 2021. I met the investor, and everything seemed to be good there. The place I thought was THE place was bought up before we could get things moving. And then out of nowhere, the investor fell through. At this point, I was supposed to be on a flight back to Louisville in four days.

We switched gears and started looking for places to rent. Place after place … none of them worked out. Two days before I was supposed to return to Louisville, I got a call from my parents warning me of an ice storm hitting Louisville; they advised me to delay my flight. I went on to check my return flight, and it wasn't set to return until the following month. God knew. Relieved that I had plenty of time to figure this out, I moved my flight to give me five more days to find a place.

Two days later I got a text from a guy I had played volleyball with on past vacations. "Hey, Juice (my volleyball nickname)! I heard you're in town. Wanna play some ball tonight?" I replied, "Man, I'd love to! But I'm in town looking for a place to rent and only have five days to find something before I leave." What I would come to find out through this exchange is that my friend was getting married and moving to Arkansas right when I was hoping to move here, which opened up his place for me to rent. And remember the talk I had with God? The specs of what I asked for… this was all of those things, but it was five minutes closer to Siesta with a pool and a hot tub. Thank you, Jesus!

Once I got there, I told myself, *I am in the season of yes*! Every invitation, every chance to meet new people, every work opportunity was a *yes*! This was everything I had always wanted, and I was going to make the most of it! The season of yes led me to meet so many fantastic people. I met my wonderful boyfriend, Wesley. I found my volleyball tribe. I built my client base and filled my calendar. I started a nonprofit with Wes called Bettering Beaches. It helped me create a life that I absolutely love!

The only problem is when there's no off switch on your season of yes, or at least a pause button, you can stretch yourself too thin. Overcommitting, overbooking, and just wearing yourself out. Especially when you're a perfectionist like I am. I don't do anything if I can't give it my all. How do you scale back from something that has led to so many wonderful things?

I learned that it doesn't have to be an all-or-nothing scenario. It's all about prioritizing saying *yes* to the things that bring you closer to the life you have envisioned for yourself. Ask yourself if this yes gets you closer to that life or might act as a distraction from it. I was having a tough time making that call on my own so now what I do is take it to God. If I feel at peace or even excited for the opportunity, it's a yes. If I feel uncertain, I pray about it, then sleep on it, ask again the following day, and then make a final call. I have learned that if I try to force something that I don't feel led to do, it almost always ends up being way more work, or an annoyance. And the things I've been at peace with end up being enjoyable, and oftentimes led to other great connections or opportunities.

So, be open to a season of yes. It takes you out of your comfort zone and opens you up to more than you can imagine. A comfort zone is just that, comfortable. But comfort zones don't stretch you, they don't challenge you. You don't really learn new things and grow in them. Know how to recognize when it's time to scale back from your season of yes, hopefully before you burn out. And I would challenge you, if you don't already have a relationship with God, to know that it's not too late to start one.

# Beyond the Blueprint: Crafting a Life with Purpose and Passion

## Carrie Riley, ASID, IIDA, NCIDQ

Carrie Riley, originally hailing from Omaha, Neb., discovered her passion for design and architecture at the young age of 16. In 2000, after earning her degree in architectural interior design, she relocated to Sarasota, Fla., to be with her soon-to-be husband and pursue fresh creative opportunities. She began her career at a prominent local firm but soon realized her desire for greater creative independence.

At just 27, Carrie took a bold leap and founded Riley Interior Design, a firm that has since become a beacon of excellence in the region. Over the past two decades, her innovative work has garnered numerous accolades, including the prestigious ASID Presidential Award, recognition as "BEST Interior Designer" by leading magazines, and a coveted spot on MSN.com's list of top 10 interior designers to follow.

Beyond her professional achievements, Carrie is a proud mother to her seven-year-old son and was an NFL Super Bowl-winning cheerleader. Known for her deep community involvement, she has earned respect not only as a visionary designer but also as a dedicated and influential member of her community.

https://www.instagram.com/carrieriley
https://www.instagram.com/rileyinteriordesign
https://www.facebook.com/carrie.mccuneriley
https://www.facebook.com/profile.php?id=100063761314676
https://www.linkedin.com/in/rileyinteriordesign/

———

Workaholic, some would say... and they wouldn't be wrong! But how do you find that elusive "work-life" balance? How do you ensure that your identity doesn't become completely tied to your career? Is it even possible to achieve success in both?

For me, my career has always been deeply personal, almost instinctual. From as early as I can remember, I knew I wanted to be a professional interior designer. There was never a Plan B or a fleeting "what if" about another career. When people ask, I often joke that I was born knowing my calling! If you ask my mom, she'd wholeheartedly agree—she loves to tell stories about my childhood passion projects.

My ultimate creation was what I called my "Barbie Dreamworld"—an entire room in our Midwest basement that I transformed into a mini city for my dolls. It wasn't just a house; it was a sprawling universe, complete with homes, shopping centers, hotels, drive-ins, and more. I'd spend countless hours designing and reimagining every detail. Thankfully, my parents supported my creative obsession. They owned a large flooring company in Omaha, Neb., and they'd bring home leftover samples—scraps of flooring, countertops, and wall coverings from their projects. Those materials became my canvas, and Barbie's world got a makeover practically every day.

Looking back, I realize how lucky I was. My parents encouraged my passion from the start, allowing me to escape into this magical, creative world. They've always been my biggest cheerleaders, and I owe so much of my journey to their unwavering support.

By the time I turned 16 and could drive, I landed a job at one of Nebraska's most prestigious high-end residential interior design firms. I started at the very bottom—and I couldn't be more grateful for that foundation. I did everything from fetching coffees and organizing fabric samples to unpacking furniture and staging showroom vignettes. I even mastered how to use a fax machine (yes, it was *that* era).

These seemingly small tasks gave me invaluable insight into how a design firm operates, layer by layer. I developed a deep appreciation for every moving part of the business, from the big-picture concepts to the tiniest details.

Balancing this job with school, being on a nationally ranked dance team, competing as a gymnast, and maintaining my grades was a challenge, to say the least. But those years taught me discipline, time management, and how to juggle competing priorities—all skills that later became critical when I launched my own firm and embarked on the entrepreneurial journey.

From the moment I set foot on the University of Nebraska's campus, I knew I was walking into one of the most challenging chapters of my life. The architecture college was renowned for its rigorous curriculum, and on the first day, the dean didn't shy away from making it clear. He stood before us and asked, *"Who here is a student-athlete? If you are, I suggest you gather your belongings now—this program demands everything, and you won't have the time to give it your all."*

I froze. My heart raced. I had dreamed of pursuing architectural interior design for as long as I could remember. I wasn't just a student-athlete—I was a co-captain of the nationally ranked Scarlet's dance team and a proud member of Kappa Kappa Gamma. Giving up wasn't an option. I stayed in my seat, vowing to prove to myself and everyone else that I could make it work. Somehow. Someway.

Those four years were a whirlwind. My days started well before dawn and often didn't end until well past 2am. Balancing the demanding architecture coursework with the physical and emotional grind of dance practices, the various sports events, charity events, and the vibrant social commitments of sorority life was nothing short of chaos. Sleep became a luxury and sacrifice a daily routine. But through the exhaustion, I learned lessons that would shape me forever—resilience, time management, and the courage to chase dreams, no matter how insurmountable they seemed.

Graduation day felt like a triumph. I held that hard-earned degree in my hands and knew I had conquered one of the most grueling challenges of my life thus far. But life wasn't about to slow down. My next chapter awaited me in Sarasota, Fla., where my soon-to-be husband had taken a position. Our story was as unexpected as it was beautiful. We'd known each other since we were 14 but didn't begin dating until my final year of college. Two weeks after we started, he moved across the country.

When I packed my bags and left for Florida, I carried more than just my belongings—I carried hope. I left behind the familiar comfort of family, friends, and the city I'd always called home. I was young and full of aspirations, entering a city where I knew no one but him. It was terrifying. It was thrilling. It was the beginning of a journey we'd navigate together, building a life with nothing but love, faith, and the promise of what could be.

Looking back, those years were the foundation for everything I've accomplished since. They weren't just about learning how to design spaces; they were about learning how to design a life filled with purpose, passion, and perseverance. Every late night, every tear shed in exhaustion, every leap of faith brought me to where I am today. And for that, I am endlessly grateful.

I began my design career in Florida at a prestigious design firm ranked among the top five in the nation. Its headquarters was based in Boca Raton, but with five design studios across the state, I was fortunate to be stationed in Sarasota. This role introduced me to the unique challenges and opportunities of designing in the South, vastly different from my Midwest roots. I quickly learned the nuances of Southern construction, architecture, and building styles, enriching my design perspective and broadening my expertise.

Not long after, I was offered an extraordinary opportunity to join a renowned architectural firm in Sarasota, celebrated for its dedication to a specific architectural style. My role was to build their interior design department from the ground up—a challenge that pushed my creativity and leadership skills to new heights. Collaborating closely with accomplished general contractors and the firm's architects, I developed a deep appreciation for the synergy required to bring clients' visions to life. This experience further honed my ability to design across a wide array of architectural styles and fostered a passion for helping clients realize their dream homes.

Moving across the country to start a professional career in a completely unfamiliar city was both thrilling and isolating. I deeply missed the sisterhood-like bonds I had left behind—my actual sister, my dance sisters, my sorority sisters, and the friends who had been part of my life since childhood. I craved connection with other young, professional women who shared my passions and interests.

Fueled by my love of dance and sports, I set my sights on an ambitious goal: becoming an NFL cheerleader for the Tampa Bay Buccaneers. The journey was exhilarating. Not only did I make the team, but I also experienced the rare and extraordinary honor of cheering during the Super Bowl and celebrating a victory with the organization. Winning the Super

Bowl was one of the most defining and unforgettable moments of my life—a dream I never imagined I'd have the privilege of living.

This incredible chapter didn't end there. Over the next 18 plus years, I cultivated a meaningful relationship with the Buccaneers, contributing as a choreographer, game day manager, and tryout coordinator, and even helping select future cheer teams. Along the way, I built lifelong friendships with the most talented, driven, and inspiring women, forming a network of support and camaraderie that continues to enrich my life.

In pursuit of professional excellence, I committed myself to earning the NCIDQ (National Council for Interior Design Qualification) certification, a milestone that defines expertise and commitment within the field. Becoming a licensed, registered interior designer in Florida is no small feat—it requires years of education, experience, and the successful completion of the rigorous NCIDQ examination. The NCIDQ certification is the gold standard in interior design, reflecting a mastery of principles that prioritize public health, safety, and welfare.

This certification not only solidifies my technical proficiency but also grants me the recognition to practice at the highest levels of the profession. It's a symbol of dedication and integrity, ensuring that my work consistently exceeds industry standards while delivering designs that are as functional as they are beautiful.

This was the true beginning of my entrepreneurial journey. At just 27 years old, armed with the confidence of having passed the rigorous NCIDQ exam, I took a bold leap of faith and founded Riley Interior Design. To say I was terrified would be an understatement, but deep down, I knew I had what it took to make it happen.

Entrepreneurship ran in my veins—my parents had owned their own business for as long as I could remember. Growing up, I watched them navigate challenges and celebrate successes, and those lessons stayed with me. During those early days of starting my own firm, I leaned heavily on my father for guidance and courage. His wisdom and encouragement became the foundation on which I built not just a business, but also a lifelong dream.

FAMILY. Yes, Jason and I had each other, and we were thriving—both running our own companies. But was that enough? From the very beginning, we always wanted children. Yet, like so many young professionals, we threw ourselves into our careers, making them the priority during our early years together. It's so easy to get caught up in the daily grind—the endless workweeks, late nights, working weekends, even holidays—all devoted to nurturing our "baby," our businesses. And before you know it, a decade has flown by.

Eventually, we refocused, setting our sights on becoming a family of three. But my mom was wrong when she said, "It only takes one time." We tried. We tried again. And again. Specialists, doctors, and countless experts—all qualified and compassionate—helped us every step of the way. Yet despite everything, we reached a point where a realist finally told us, "This may not be in the cards for you."

So, we redirected. We had to. We made the hard decision to pour ourselves fully into our work, accepting that our careers might be the only "baby" we'd ever have. But what if that wasn't enough? Life offers a small window of opportunity, and if you miss it, it's gone forever. We knew that. And still, we buried our heads, avoided the difficult conversations, and just kept working. Until two life-altering moments happened for both Jason and me. The hard truth of wanting children became even more clear... so, we redirected again. And started our new journey: our adoption journey and the journey to not only pursue a family of three but maintain my original "baby": my career and the work-life balance of it all.

Fast-forward seven years, and here we are. I've now owned Riley Interior Design for over 20 years, and I thank God every single day for the incredible journey it has been. My business is thriving, allowing me to work on some of the most extraordinary projects alongside phenomenal clients, architects, general contractors, and truly remarkable individuals.

While I absolutely love my firm, my career, and the people I get to collaborate with, the greatest joy and blessing of my life is our seven-year-old son. I honestly don't know how I lived before his arrival. He is an absolute piece of my heart—a constant reminder of how profoundly life can change when someone becomes your everything. From the moment I first held him in my arms, it was as if my entire world shifted, and his needs became my greatest priority. It's amazing how God knows exactly what you need, even before you do.

Our adoption story is deeply meaningful, but it's also his story to tell when he's ready. Perhaps one day I'll share it in a sequel book. For now, my focus is on being the best mother I can be and showing him, through example, how to build a life and career that you love. I want him to see the joy in waking up each day excited about what you get to do. That's the life I've built, and it's the legacy I hope to pass on to him.

# Transforming Lives: My Journey in Aesthetic Medicine and Community Impact

Jessica Simone

**Meet Jessica Simone, APRN: Your Partner in Confidence and Wellness**

Jessica Simone, MSN, AGNP-C, is a board-certified adult and gerontology nurse practitioner with a passion for aesthetic and integrative medicine. She holds a BSN from the University of Connecticut and a master's degree from South University and is credentialed by the American Academy of Nurse Practitioners. As an Evexias Health certified provider and an active member of A4M, the American Med Spa Association, and the American Academy of Facial Aesthetics, Jessica combines advanced medical expertise with a dedication to enhancing natural beauty and overall wellness.

As the founder of Harmony Med Spa, Jessica leads a team of skilled professionals in delivering transformative treatments within a peaceful and inviting atmosphere. With a holistic approach, she offers a wide range of services, including advanced laser therapies, custom facials, and medically supervised weight loss programs. Jessica's philosophy revolves around empowering each client to feel confident and radiant, both inside and out. She tailors every treatment plan to the unique needs and goals of each individual, ensuring an experience that is both personal and rejuvenating.

Known for her integrative approach, Jessica stays at the forefront of the latest advancements in aesthetic and wellness treatments. Whether it's balancing hormones with bioidentical hormone replacement therapy (BHRT), kickstarting weight loss with peptide therapy, or offering subtle aesthetic enhancements like Botox® and dermal fillers, Jessica empowers her patients to feel unstoppable. Her expertise, gained through training with industry leaders like Galderma, Merz, and Allergan, ensures exceptional care.

Don't miss a moment—stay connected and see the transformations, tips, and behind-the-scenes magic happening daily on Instagram: @jessicasimonenp.

Facebook: Harmony Med Spa
Instagram: @HarmonyMedSpa_fl
www.harmonymedspafl.com

———

Life has a way of presenting us with opportunities that shape who we become, and for me, that journey began in the unlikeliest of places: the U.S. Army. From there, my medical career evolved in ways I never imagined, taking me from serving as an Army medic to becoming a board-certified nurse practitioner with a passion for aesthetic medicine. Today, I have the privilege of transforming lives by helping individuals look and feel their best through a holistic approach to wellness and advanced aesthetic care. As the founder of Harmony Med Spa, I'm proud to share my journey of making a mark in this incredible city by blending medical expertise, artistry, and a passion for empowering others.

## From Army Medic to Healing Touch

Serving in the military laid the foundation for everything I would later accomplish. As an Army medic, I was trained to think quickly, act decisively, and always put the needs of others first. But what I came to realize over time was that while I loved the fast-paced, hands-on nature of medicine, I longed to dive deeper into the art of healing. The Army gave me the skills and the discipline to succeed, but my journey into the world of healthcare was just beginning.

Thanks to the military, I earned my bachelor of science in nursing (BSN) and spent years working in various roles at the Tampa Veterans Hospital. From the clinical floors to quality management, I saw firsthand the complexities of healthcare. However, after eight years of working as a registered nurse, I felt a strong pull to do more. I wanted to move beyond just managing symptoms; I wanted to empower my patients to heal and thrive. That's when I set my sights on becoming a nurse practitioner, allowing me to take on a more proactive and impactful role in patient care.

## The Evolution: Aesthetic Medicine and Regenerative Therapies

Once I became a nurse practitioner, I discovered a field that truly ignited my passion: aesthetic and regenerative therapies. With eight years of clinical experience, I've built a strong foundation in healthcare, which allows me to combine that knowledge with my love for aesthetic medicine. For the past five years, I've dedicated myself to rejuvenating and enhancing my patients' appearance—and, more importantly, their confidence. Aesthetic medicine goes far beyond just Botox and fillers; it's about helping people become the best versions of themselves, both inside and out.

At the core of my work is my belief that beauty and wellness go hand in hand. I'm honored to offer advanced treatments such as Botox, dermal fillers, PDO thread lifts, laser skin rejuvenation, and other facial therapies to restore youthful vibrancy and enhance natural beauty. But the work I do is never just about physical appearance—it's about creating a safe, nurturing space where my patients feel comfortable, valued, and seen. My approach is to make each treatment a personalized experience, ensuring that every person receives the care and attention they deserve.

Whether smoothing fine lines with Botox, restoring volume with dermal fillers, or rejuvenating skin with laser therapies, my goal is to help my patients not just look better but feel better about who they are. I love seeing how a subtle enhancement can completely transform a person's self-esteem and outlook on life, helping them feel refreshed, confident, and ready to take on the world.

One of the aspects I love most about my work is the transformation that goes far beyond the physical. For example, I worked with a woman who came to me devastated after undergoing extensive dental work that caused significant, unintended weight loss. The dental procedure affected her ability to eat properly, leading to drastic changes in her facial appearance. She lost volume in her cheeks, and the changes were so noticeable that she felt self-conscious and uncomfortable in her own skin. She expressed how she used to feel vibrant and confident, but now, she avoided social gatherings and even struggled to look at herself in the mirror.

After a thorough consultation, we created a personalized treatment plan that included a combination of dermal fillers, RF microneedling and Sculptra, to restore lost volume, tighten the skin, and rebalance her facial contours. As we progressed through each session, I saw her transformation unfold—not just physically but emotionally. She started regaining the fullness and natural contours of her face, and with that, her confidence resurfaced.

The change wasn't just about the aesthetics; it was about restoring her sense of self. As she regained the youthful appearance she once had, she also rediscovered the strength and vitality she had lost along the way. She went from feeling invisible and defeated to being excited about re-engaging in her social life. Her smile became genuine again, and she was no longer hiding from the world.

## A Holistic Approach: Healing from the Inside Out

But my expertise isn't confined to just enhancing beauty on the surface. I believe that true wellness begins within, and that's why I'm also deeply committed to helping my patients achieve optimal health through treatments like bioidentical hormone replacement therapy (BHRT) and peptide therapy. These therapies aren't just about looking good—they're about feeling good and preventing the breakdown of the body over time.

One memorable patient, a 58-year-old male who was struggling with high blood pressure, cholesterol issues, and insulin resistance, was able to turn his life around after working with me on balancing his hormones and addressing his weight. Through personalized care, healthy weight loss, and hormone optimization, he got off all medications and reclaimed his vitality. Stories like these inspire me every day and drive me to continuously seek out new ways to help people not just look younger but feel younger and healthier as well.

The most rewarding part of my journey has been witnessing the transformations—both physical and emotional—that our clients experience. One client who stands out came to us feeling defeated after years of struggling with weight and fatigue. Through our GLP-1 program and metabolic repair plan, she not only lost 40 pounds but also regained her confidence and zest for life.

## A Heart for the Community: Giving Back to Sarasota

While my work in aesthetic and integrative medicine has allowed me to help individuals achieve life-changing results, my commitment to Sarasota extends far beyond my practice. I believe that a strong community is built not only by providing exceptional services but by giving back and being an active participant in the lives of those around us.

I'm proud to be deeply involved in several community initiatives, from supporting local charities to sponsoring events that have a lasting impact. Harmony Med Spa is a proud sponsor of the American Cancer Society. We are excited to know that our contribution helps raise awareness and funds for life-saving cancer research. We also believe strongly in supporting our local schools and animal shelters—after all, the future of Sarasota depends on the care we show to our children and the compassion we offer to all living beings.

Through my involvement in the southwest Florida BNI (Business Network International) chapter, I collaborate with other small business owners to foster growth and prosperity in Sarasota and Lakewood Ranch. Together, we create an ecosystem of support, helping one another build stronger, more connected businesses that contribute to the overall health and well-being of the community.

## The Power of Connection: Patients as Partners

The relationships I build with my patients are at the heart of everything I do. I don't just see them as patients; I see them as partners in their health journey. Whether they come to me for facial balancing or hormone therapy, I take the time to listen to their concerns, understand their goals, and develop a personalized treatment plan that aligns with their needs.

What excites me the most is the ability to grow alongside my patients. We're in this together, and the progress we make is something I celebrate with them. It's not just about the immediate results—it's about the long-term benefits and the confidence my patients gain as they continue their journey toward optimal health and well-being.

For example, a patient came to me with concerns about her facial appearance as she aged. After several treatments, she not only saw the physical changes but also gained a renewed sense of confidence that extended into her professional life and personal relationships. I watched her transform from someone who had been avoiding events and hiding from cameras into a woman who embraced her newfound self-esteem. Moments like these remind me why I do what I do: to help people feel like the best versions of themselves.

## Looking to the Future: A Legacy of Health and Transformation

As I look toward the future, my mission remains clear: to be the go-to provider for aesthetic treatments, health optimization, and transformational care in Sarasota. I strive to be someone people can count on—not just for the services I provide, but for the genuine care and dedication I bring to every interaction.

My work in aesthetic medicine is just one part of a larger vision—one where health, beauty, and confidence are accessible to everyone. I believe that through education, personalized care, and a holistic approach to wellness, we can make a lasting impact on the lives of those in our community.

When it comes to making a difference, I'm committed to doing more than just offering treatments—I'm here to offer solutions, encouragement, and the support needed to truly thrive. Whether it's through helping someone regain their youthful appearance, assisting with hormone optimization, or contributing to causes that uplift our community, I am passionate about being a part of something bigger than myself.

This is just the beginning. The best is yet to come, and I am excited for the many lives we'll continue to transform together.

## Leading the Future of Wellness and Aesthetics

The fields of wellness and aesthetic medicine are ever-evolving, and I'm passionate about staying at the forefront of innovation. From exploring new technologies in regenerative medicine to expanding services like peptide therapy and advanced aesthetic treatments, I am committed to bringing the best to my clients.

Looking ahead, I envision Harmony Med Spa continuing to grow as a trusted cornerstone in Sarasota for both aesthetic and wellness care. I am committed to ensuring Harmony remains a symbol of excellence and a source of confidence for all who walk through our doors.

## A Message to Sarasota

To the people of Sarasota: Thank you for welcoming me and allowing me to be part of this extraordinary community. Your stories, resilience, and support inspire me every day.

As I reflect on my journey, I am filled with gratitude—for the clients who trust me, the team who stands beside me, and the city that has embraced me. Being featured in *Slaying Sarasota* is a milestone, but it's also a reminder that this is just the beginning. I am excited to continue making my mark in Sarasota and beyond, one transformation at a time.

# From Garage Beginnings to Global AI Innovator

## Florencia Tarque

Florencia Tarque is a visionary in AI, renowned for designing transformative systems that automate, optimize, and revolutionize business operations. With a global clientele acquired entirely through referrals—without marketing, advertising, or a website—Florencia exemplifies the power of delivering exceptional results that speak for themselves.

Her big break came with injecting AI into recruiting, showcasing AI's potential to revolutionize traditional industries. Building on this success, Florencia delivers solutions to businesses of all kinds, tackling bottlenecks in operations, sales, HR, finance, and customer service. She also brings entrepreneurs' ideas to life, creating MVPs (minimum viable products) that transform visions into reality.

A sales expert and networking strategist, Florencia is frequently flown to global conventions to connect with leaders and share insights. As a business growth consultant, she boasts a dynamic international and domestic portfolio.

Her expertise extends to centralizing data, streamlining workflows, and delivering real-time insights to empower smarter decisions and sustainable growth. Designed to adapt and grow with businesses, her solutions future-proof organizations in a rapidly evolving digital landscape.

Known as the go-to expert for solving the impossible, Florencia's bespoke solutions and global network ensure businesses not only survive but thrive in the age of AI. In her free time? Modeling and traveling the world. You can see her journey on Instagram @IfYouKnowFlo!

———

I didn't grow up in a high-rise penthouse or even a cozy suburban home. Nope. I grew up in a garage. My parents, immigrants chasing the American Dream, were too busy working multiple jobs to pull us out of it, so my grandmother stepped in to raise me. My parents' grind eventually paid off—they built a successful business in California, and for a while, life felt stable. That is, until 2008 when everything came crashing down. We lost it all and relocated to Lancaster, South Carolina—a culture shock that felt like moving to another planet.

In Lancaster, I was "the outsider," navigating a new world where I didn't quite fit. To cope, I turned to sports. I joined soccer, basketball (despite never having played), and—because why not?—football. I became the only girl in South Carolina playing wide receiver, which attracted a lot of attention... good and bad. My car got egged, I was bullied online, and girls delighted in making my life hell. Instead of retreating, I fought back by launching an anti-bullying campaign called "End the Hate," which landed me on Fox News. By the time I graduated, I'd earned high honors, a first-generation college scholarship, and, miraculously, a solid reputation in a town that once felt alien.

But life didn't get easier. In college, just as finals loomed, I found myself homeless when my friend bailed and left me couch-less. I spent that week living in my car with my dog, wondering how I'd make it through. Necessity breeds ingenuity, right? I rented some cleaning equipment, started scrubbing dorms and apartments, and turned it into a full-blown business. I even built a basic scheduling app so students could book online. That cleaning hustle not only kept me afloat but also marked the beginning of my entrepreneurial journey.

Fast forward to 2019, and I was working a mind-numbing recruiting job in Orlando, barely making ends meet. Then, one day, I tested an AI model and asked about a virus in China. Its prediction? The world would shut down in six months. That afternoon, I quit my job, moved back home, and waited. March 2020 rolled around, and—surprise!—the world shut down. With nothing but time on my hands, I dove headfirst into AI.

It wasn't smooth sailing. For two years, I wrestled with imposter syndrome, wondering if I'd bitten off more than I could chew. But I kept pushing, eventually building a business that would change everything. My breakthrough came with AI recruiting systems. I saw how businesses struggled with hiring inefficiencies and turnover, so I built systems that were automated, cost-effective, and hands-off. Whether for global call centers, U.S.-based 1099 reps, or W2 employees, my systems simplified the entire process—from sourcing to onboarding—without anyone needing to wade through resumes or endure endless interviews. Think of it as recruiting on autopilot, freeing up managers to focus on what actually matters.

And it wasn't just recruiting. My AI solutions tackled inefficiencies across operations, sales, HR, finance, and customer service. They centralized data, flipped call-center dialers on turbo, streamlined workflows, took over training, and provided real-time analytics to improve decision-making, just to name a few. The best part? They're scalable and user-friendly, requiring minimal technical expertise. Businesses loved that they could grow without the headaches, and I loved delivering solutions that truly made an impact, helping businesses and entrepreneurs all over the world with an AI solution to any bottleneck within their business.

As my solutions gained traction, so did my network. Somewhere along the way, I became *that person*. Need an acquisition? I'll make the connection. Sourcing talent in Dubai? I got you. Need to fill a call center and automate? No problem. Want to train your sales reps with life-like scenarios? Done! My global network opened doors others couldn't even knock on, and I earned a reputation as the go-to for the impossible.

Today, I've built a life I once dreamed about. I've faced my share of wild moments—like almost getting kidnapped in Mexico or surviving a heart attack at 29—but I've never let setbacks define me. I've lived in five countries, traveled to over 10 in the last year alone, and work on my terms. My systems don't just automate businesses—they free people, just like they've freed me.

If there's one thing I've learned, it's that you don't need a perfect start or a foolproof plan. You need grit, a sense of humor, and the willingness to roll with the punches. If I can go from a garage to building world-class AI systems while globe-trotting, so can anyone else. I am, therefore I can. Now say it again and believe it, because I believe in you.

# Turning Setbacks into Success

## Giuliana Vann

Giuliana Vann is the CEO of Living a Digital Dream, an award-winning boutique agency specializing in social media management, content creation, and branding. Originally from Lima, Peru, Giuliana embarked on her transformative journey at 17, moving to the United States in pursuit of a brighter future. After a sports injury shifted her career path from nursing to digital marketing, she discovered her passion for helping business owners and entrepreneurs grow their brands through the power of social media.

Giuliana has transformed the lives of over 100 business owners and entrepreneurs, globally, enhancing their visibility, growing their brands and businesses, and increasing their brand awareness through her coaching programs, the Instapreneur Success, a leading program, and managing their social media accounts and helping thousands of others through her courses and free tips online.

Driven by a desire to uplift others, Giuliana uses her Instagram expertise to inspire entrepreneurs, business owners, and influencers to embrace their unique stories and authenticity, empower them through the power of resilience, and pursue their dreams. She believes that every setback is an opportunity for growth and encourages her clients to take bold steps toward their goals.

Giuliana's journey is a testament to the power of resilience and the impact of believing in oneself. As she continues to grow and evolve, she remains dedicated to creating a legacy of empowerment, inspiring others to chase their dreams and make their mark on the world.

Instagram: @giulianavann and @livingadigitaldream
https://www.livingadigitaldream.com/

————

I often reflect on my journey and the myriad of experiences that have shaped me into the woman I am today. As the CEO of Living a Digital Dream, an award-winning boutique social media marketing agency specializing in social media management, content creation, and branding, I have learned invaluable lessons that extend far beyond the realm of business. These lessons are not just about achieving success; they are about personal growth, resilience, and the unwavering belief in oneself.

My story began in Lima, Peru, where I dreamed of a future filled with opportunities. At the age of 17, I decided to leave my home and embark on a new adventure in the United States with my mom. This decision was driven by a desire to create a bright future for myself. The transition was not easy; I faced cultural barriers, language challenges, and the uncertainty that comes with starting a new life in a foreign land. But through it all, I discovered the power of believing in myself. My faith also helped me go through those challenging moments as I was trying to figure out what to do for my life. I knew I wanted to help others somehow and getting into the medical field made sense.

So, the path to achieving my education goals started. I got my GED and my associate of arts degree to apply to nursing school. With my 4.0 GPA, I was on the dean's list and in the honors society in college. In December 2011, I graduated with my associate's degree in nursing, and in January 2012, I started my first nursing job at one of the local hospitals as a day shift nurse in the medical-surgical/oncology unit. During my five-year nursing career, I rapidly scaled and became a charge nurse and a nursing preceptor. Every time I mentored a nurse, I felt something special; it was then that I realized I really enjoyed mentoring others.

In early 2017, life threw me a curveball with a sports injury to my ankle. That March, I had to have surgery, which forced me to reevaluate the path of my nursing job at the hospital. Meanwhile, I managed to complete my bachelor's in nursing while recovering from a challenging surgery and with a seven-month-old baby and a four-year-old at home. Two months later, I walked onto the stage on crutches to receive my bachelor's diploma. I faced a long road ahead recovering from surgery and had to learn how to walk again.

I knew at that point that going back to 14-hour shifts at the hospital was not possible due to my lack of mobility. Meanwhile, my passion for social media had been reignited. Deep inside, I knew God had a new plan for me. It was a challenging period, but it also became a pivotal moment of transformation.

During those tough times, I never let these setbacks prevent me from pushing forward; I realized that they were not failures, but opportunities for growth. Each obstacle became a stepping stone guiding me toward a new path.

While I was at home recovering, I took massive action—an essential first step toward creating a life that aligns with your passions and aspirations. I started building my personal brand on social media, and within a year grew a community of over 20,000 followers on Instagram, all by sharing my story and staying authentic to myself. I only posted on a single platform, and I only posted a few days a week.

People started asking me to coach them to grow their brands on Instagram, and that's when I knew I was onto something: I figured I could leverage my passion and my following to help people, and show them that you absolutely *can* build a successful brand by using a streamlined, time-efficient strategy. After founding my social media agency a year later (at the start of the pandemic), I built a six-figure coaching and agency business and was recognized as one of the 40 Business Leaders under 40 in the Gulf Coast of Florida. My agency won Best of Florida in the Digital Marketing Firm category in 2023 and 2024.

Resilience taught me to adapt and thrive in the face of adversity. I embraced the mindset that every challenge is an opportunity to learn and evolve. This perspective has been instrumental in my journey, allowing me to rise stronger after each setback. I often remind myself that true strength lies not in avoiding difficulties but in facing them head-on and emerging victorious.

A strong mindset is a powerful tool in navigating the complexities of life. I have made it a priority to cultivate positivity and gratitude in my daily life. Every morning, I take time for meditation, allowing myself to center my thoughts and set intentions for the day. This practice has been transformative, providing clarity and focus as I tackle the challenges ahead.

Staying positive is not about ignoring the negatives; it's about acknowledging them while choosing to focus on the possibilities. I've learned to reframe my thoughts and see obstacles as opportunities for growth. This shift in perspective has propelled me forward, enabling me to maintain a sense of hope and optimism, even in the face of uncertainty.

I embrace the mindset of lifelong learning, recognizing that knowledge is power. This is a non-negotiable in my field, because the social media landscape evolves so quickly; to give my best, I must stay on top of all the latest trends and updates while upleveling my marketing and business acumen. This is the most important investment I can make in myself, which benefits my business and my clients. Every book I read, every workshop I attend, and every mentor I connect with contributes to growth.

Investing in myself has opened doors to new opportunities and equipped me with the tools I need to excel in my career. The more I learn, the more I can share with others. I've made it my mission to empower fellow entrepreneurs and aspiring influencers with the insights I've gained. Through my coaching program, the Instapreneur Success Program, and my professional social media management services managing multiple social media accounts, I have had the privilege of helping over 100 businesses grow their online presence. Each success story reinforces my belief that knowledge shared is knowledge multiplied.

I cannot emphasize enough the importance of daily habits in my journey. Taking care of my body and mind has been essential to my overall well-being and success. I prioritize hitting the gym consistently three to five times a week, recognizing that physical health directly impacts mental clarity and productivity. Exercise is my outlet; it energizes me and provides a much-needed break from the hustle of entrepreneurship.

In addition to fitness, my daily morning meditation has become a sacred ritual. It's a time for reflection, gratitude, and intention-setting. These habits create a solid foundation for my day, helping me approach challenges with a clear mind and positive energy. I encourage others to cultivate their daily rituals, as they can be transformative in achieving personal and professional goals.

As I navigate the ups and downs of entrepreneurship, I always remind myself to look at the big picture. It is easy to get caught up in the hustle and bustle of daily tasks, but I strive to keep my vision in focus. When faced with failures or obstacles that seem insurmountable, I take a step back and remind myself of why I started this journey in the first place.

I've learned that persistence is key. There were moments when I felt overwhelmed and questioned my decisions. In those times, I leaned into my faith, passion, and the belief that my dreams were worth pursuing. I remind myself that every successful person has faced failures; it's the refusal to give up that sets them apart. I encourage anyone on a similar path to embrace their dreams fully and never lose sight of the vision they hold for themselves.

Taking massive action has been one of the most significant catalysts for my growth. I've learned that waiting for the perfect moment often leads to missed opportunities. Instead, I embrace the belief that you will never feel entirely ready; the key is to start. Whether it's launching a new initiative, trying out a new marketing strategy, or networking with industry leaders, I dive in headfirst.

This approach has generated momentum in my life and career. Each action, no matter how small, builds upon itself and creates a ripple effect of positive change. I often share this principle with my clients and mentees, urging them to take that first step, no matter how daunting it may seem. It's through action that we gain clarity, confidence, and the ability to adapt and grow.

I'm proud of how far I've come and the success I've achieved. But ultimately, my journey is about uplifting others and leaving a legacy. Mentoring others in nursing school ignited my passion for helping others, and I carry that on today through my work in social media. I see each client, each mentee, and each connection as part of a larger community. My marketing expertise and unique strategic approach help businesses authentically build and scale their brand presence and grow their communities. I believe that when we empower one another, we create a ripple effect that can transform lives.

When clients come to me, they stay because they are satisfied with how their brand presence looks and sounds: like them, but better. This leads to tangible results of increased engagement and revenue. I spend plenty of time getting a deep understanding of each client's unique brand, brand voice, and goals and developing custom strategies based on my client research and my own tested methods. I then create compelling copy in the client's voice, which enhances their brand identity and boosts engagement. Clear communication and collaboration are always essential for achieving the best possible results.

As I continue to grow and evolve, I remain committed to sharing my knowledge and experiences. I want to inspire women and aspiring entrepreneurs to embrace their unique voices and share their stories with the world. I encourage them to believe in themselves, cultivate resilience, and take action toward their goals. Together, we can create a community of empowered individuals who are not afraid to chase their dreams and support one another along the way.

My journey is far from over. I wake up every day with renewed enthusiasm, ready to tackle new challenges and seize opportunities. Each day is a chance to learn, grow, and make a difference. I am continually inspired by the stories of those around me, and I am committed to being a source of inspiration for others.

As I reflect on my path, I am grateful for the experiences that have shaped me. I have learned that the act of believing in myself is not a one-time event; it is a continuous journey. I embrace the ups and downs, knowing that they are all part of life.

I invite you to join me on this journey of growth and empowerment. Let's celebrate our victories, learn from our failures, and uplift one another as we navigate the ever-evolving landscape of life and business. Together, we can leave our mark, create a legacy of empowerment, and inspire future generations of women to embrace their dreams fearlessly.

So, to anyone reading this, know that you have the power within you to shape your own story. Believe in yourself, cultivate resilience, and take massive action. The world is waiting for your unique voice and your incredible skills. Let's slay together!

# From ACEs to Advocacy: The Making of a Relentless Protector

## Leanndra Yates, M. Ed.

Leanndra Yates is a lifelong advocate for children, families, and education, driven by a personal mission to create safe, supportive environments where every child can thrive. Adopted from Chile as an infant, Leanndra's early experiences shaped her passion for equity and justice, inspiring a career defined by compassion, resilience, and an unyielding commitment to advocacy.

With over a decade of experience in education, Leanndra has served as a teacher, administrator, and mentor, always striving to protect and uplift the most vulnerable. Her work has impacted countless lives, from the students in her classrooms to the families she now serves through *Exclusive Insights*, the education consultancy business she founded. Guided by her belief that every child deserves a champion, Leanndra provides expert support to families navigating the education systems, ensuring their voices are heard and their rights are respected.

Leanndra's contributions extend beyond her consultancy. She is the president of *Mind, Body, Spirit Education*, a nonprofit dedicated to holistic approaches to learning. She serves on the board of an innovative private school, *Star Lab*, also in Sarasota. As a wife to her high school sweetheart and a mother of two, Leanndra's personal and professional lives reflect her values of connection, education, and empowerment.

In her debut book, *Safe Spaces, Strong Minds: Nurturing Mental Wellness in Educational Environments*, set to release in 2025, Leanndra shares her expertise on the importance of psychological safety in schools. Through her writing, she aims to inspire educators, parents, and advocates to reimagine what is possible for children everywhere.

www.LeanndraYates.com
www.ExclusiveInsights.org
www.MindBodySpiritEduction.org
www.Instagram.com/LeanndraYates
https://leanndrayates.bsky.social

———

I carry my past like a worn map tucked into my back pocket—a guide, a warning, a testament to the roads I've traveled. My story isn't something I parade out for sympathy or to say, *Look what I've endured.* It's simply a part of me, woven into the fabric of who I've become: a protector, an advocate, a relentless force for the marginalized. My past reminds me how to navigate the world—when to speak up, when to stay quiet, and when to disappear.

My childhood was a storm of adverse experiences—physical, sexual, and emotional abuse, and living in a home with a mentally ill caregiver who developed brain cancer and became cognitively and physically disabled. There weren't enough protective adults to shield me, so I grew up fast. Too fast.

Inside our home, I cooked frozen meals for myself and my adoptive mother, who was dealing with her mental illness and the aftermath of her cancer treatments. My father, overwhelmed as a single parent and breadwinner, didn't learn about the abuse until the day he caught her striking me with her cane. His fury was immediate and protective. That was the first time I realized someone could stand up for me.

My father sacrificed everything—his social life, his dream career, and the traditional upbringing he'd known, where divorce was taboo. His love was unshakable, his dedication unmatched. He was the only person in my life who always saw me and claimed me as his—to him, I was never "the adopted one." He wasn't just my protector; he was my rock. He taught me to fight back when the world was cruel but also to trust that I was worth fighting for. He showed me that love is steadfast, even when life is relentless.

When he remarried, my stepmother brought a new dimension to my life. She had endured unimaginable abuse at the hands of her father and ex-husband, emerging from that darkness with a resilience that inspired me. She encouraged me to find my voice—not to shrink but to grow, to protect myself, and, just as importantly, to let the right people into my life. She showed me that strength and vulnerability could coexist. Her wisdom laid the foundation for my most significant relationships, including the one with my partner.

Meeting at 14 and 16, my partner and I have grown together in ways I never thought possible. We've stumbled, learned, and evolved side by side, creating a bond that is unbreakable. He knows me better than anyone, seeing my scars and strengths equally. He empowers, supports, and loves me unconditionally, meeting me as an equal in every sense.

But outside our home, the world was still a battlefield. In our tiny town, with its single stoplight, I learned the meaning of discrimination. "Hey, you dropped your green card!" they'd sneer, even though I didn't fully understand what it meant, nor was it even relevant. They called me slurs for Spanish-speaking people, mocked my Chilean heritage, and teased me for my adoptive mother's disabilities. The hatred was relentless.

Growing up in the Mennonite community, service was the ultimate virtue. "Put others first," they said. *Be small. Be quiet. Be humble.* I tried, but being small and quiet didn't protect me from the chaos. Youth group and school should have been a haven. Instead, it became a cage. Boys felt entitled to my body, commenting on it, and touching me without consequence. *My* small-town religious teachings told me to endure, to serve, to only speak up when injustice was severe enough to merit it. I endured, but inside, I felt rage. My father, in his quietly rebellious way, had taught me to physically defend myself when needed. I did, once. When I was nine, a classmate unzipped his jacket and pretended to strip in front of me in class; I slapped him hard enough to leave a welt on his face. When the teacher returned to the room, no one shared my classmates' inappropriate actions or my response.

A few weeks later, during recess, I learned what happens when you defend yourself. Three boys held me down while another assaulted me. I never stood up for myself again—not because I was weak, but because the fallout from seeking adult protection that day was unbearable. I learned to dissociate, laugh off inappropriateness, and never resist when someone wanted access to me; I learned to retreat in silence.

Yet, in that silence, seeds of resilience were planted.

As I grew older, I found solace in teaching. In undergrad, I absorbed the belief that every child carries invisible battles, and my classroom could be a safe harbor. I poured my heart into creating environments where children could express themselves, fail safely, and grow. I was determined to be the protective factor I didn't have.

When I became a mother, my empathy expanded tenfold. My children taught me new ways to lead and love. By 2017, I had earned a master's degree and was leading school communities. I served my colleagues with the same fervor I served my students, recognizing that protecting teachers meant protecting children.

My work with Exclusive Insights is a natural extension of the protector I've always been. For families navigating the complexities of education, I am the person who walks into the fire with them. I use my lived experiences, my professional expertise, and my unrelenting determination to fight battles on behalf of the children and parents who feel voiceless.

I know what it means to have the odds stacked against you, to stand at the crossroads of advocacy and bureaucracy, and to wonder if anyone is truly in your corner. That's why I am a force to be reckoned with. I hold school systems accountable, ensuring that every child's right to learn in a safe, supportive environment is honored. I champion parents who need someone to amplify their voices, strategize, and push when the system pushes back.

Each client's story becomes part of mine. I fiercely advocate because I see every angle and every layer of complexity. My role is not just about solutions—it's about ensuring families know they have someone standing with them, fighting for them. I refuse to let any child endure the helplessness I once felt in places deemed "safe," and I will move mountains to ensure they have what they need to thrive.

But it wasn't until 2023 that I truly found myself. I traveled to the country where I was born and reignited a passion and love that I didn't know existed.

That March, I traveled to Chile for the first time. It wasn't just a trip; it was a homecoming. My partner and I packed up our family of four and flew across the world to meet my biological brother and his family. When we arrived, playful and grounding, he repeatedly told me, "Tranquilla, tranquilla," sensing my nervous energy as if he had known me my whole life. Seven years of video calls couldn't prepare me for the overwhelming connection I felt when I stepped onto Chilean soil.

The mountains surrounding Santiago felt like a protective embrace. The air smelled of earth and eucalyptus, mingling with the aroma of empanadas baking in corner ovens. My biological mother greeted me with open arms as we stepped off the plane, her face lined with the same stories etched into mine.

My brother and I hiked together every day, our children laughing and bonding despite the language barrier. We shared meals, explored the land, and exchanged pieces of our lives. For the first time, I felt what it meant to belong unconditionally.

Chile awakened something in me—a connection to Llalin Kushe, the Mapuche symbol of wisdom, strength, and protection. Llalin Kushe embodies everything I strive to be. She is the grandmother, the warrior, the guardian. Her essence resonates in the path I've walked and the choices I've made.

I am no longer the girl who feels invisible, nor am I just the survivor of adverse childhood experiences. I am the woman who speaks out when others are silent. I am the protector, the advocate, the bridge between worlds. My past is not a weight; it's my compass. It reminds me of where I've been and how far I've come.

As I use my voice for psychological safety and justice, I know I'm not just slaying the demons of my past—I'm slaying the obstacles for every child and adult who needs someone to stand beside them. This is who I am. And this is just the beginning.

# Climbing Confidence: One Step at a Time

## Simone Knego

Simone Knego is an international speaker, award-winning author, and life coach dedicated to inspiring women to embrace their authentic selves. As the bestselling author of *The Extraordinary UnOrdinary You* and co-host of the globally ranked podcast Her Unshakeable Confidence with her daughter, Olivia, Simone shares transformative stories of self-discovery, resilience, and overcoming self-doubt. A two-time TEDx

Speaker, her work has been featured on ABC, NBC, CBS, *Entrepreneur Magazine*, and Yahoo News. Her writing has received numerous accolades, including the National Indie Excellence Award and the NYC Big Book Award.

Simone's transformative REAL Method—Respect your reflection, Embrace your failures, Ask yourself what you want, and Love the woman in the mirror—guides women to shift their mindset, reconnect with their confidence, and lead more fulfilling lives. Central to her approach is the belief that when you change how you see yourself, the world around you changes. This philosophy resonates deeply in her coaching and keynote presentations, empowering high-achieving women to overcome self-doubt and rediscover their extraordinary potential.

Beyond her professional achievements, Simone's life is a testament to her teachings. She has summited Mt. Kilimanjaro, raised six children, and nurtured a 31-year marriage alongside three lively dogs. Simone's warmth, humor, and authenticity shine through in every aspect of her work, inspiring women worldwide to embrace their journeys, love the woman in the mirror, and realize the power they hold within.

LinkedIn @simoneknego
Instagram @simoneknego
Facebook @speakersimoneknego

———

I stood at the base of Mount Kilimanjaro, 8,000 miles from home, staring at the mountain that had dominated my thoughts for the past six months. Its summit rose 19,341 feet into the sky, the fourth-highest in the world.

As I craned my neck to see the top, I felt my confidence take a nosedive.

What was I doing here?

Did I seriously think I could climb this?

Let me paint the picture for you: I live in Florida, a state that's essentially as flat as a pancake. My house is 12 feet above sea level. The highest hill in Florida? Just 345 feet. And here I was, standing at the base of Kilimanjaro, staring up at a mountain that was 56 times taller.

I'd spent months training—hiking, walking with a weighted backpack, and even using the StairMaster, which I despise. But none of that mattered as I stood there. Self-doubt stormed in like an unwelcome guest, planting thoughts like:

"You're not a real climber."

"You're a mom of six—you have no business being here."

"You're going to fail, and everyone will see it."

But I'd made a promise—to myself and to the Livestrong Foundation. This climb wasn't just a personal challenge; it was for a cause bigger than me. And if there's one thing I don't do, it's back out of a commitment.

So, I took a deep breath, adjusted my pack, and put one foot in front of the other.

## The Battle Within

Climbing a mountain like Kilimanjaro isn't just a physical challenge—it's a mental one. Each day brought new terrain, new obstacles, and new opportunities for my inner critic to rear its ugly head.

On the fifth day, we reached the final stretch. We began our ascent at 11:00 p.m., hiking through the pitch-black night with headlamps lighting the narrow trail. The air was so thin it felt like every breath took twice the effort. My legs screamed for rest, my lungs burned, and exhaustion weighed on me like a lead blanket.

And then came the doubts—the loudest they'd been all week:

"You're too old for this."

"You're not strong enough."

"You're going to fail."

It felt like a chorus of negativity was playing on repeat in my head. Every step was a fight—not just against the mountain, but against myself.

Still, I kept going. One step. Then another.

## The Moment Everything Changed

Hours later, just as the first rays of sunlight peeked over the horizon, I caught sight of the summit. The sky turned a brilliant shade of blue, the snow sparkled in the morning light, and for a moment, time seemed to stop.

I pushed through the final switchback, tears streaming down my face as I reached the top. There, a weathered wooden sign greeted me:

**CONGRATULATIONS! You are now at UHURU Peak, Tanzania. Africa's highest point.**

I took out my phone—more out of habit than expectation— and found the impossible: three bars of service. I called home, and chaos erupted on the other end. My husband answered, and I could hear the kids cheering, the dogs barking, and everyone talking over each other.

It was beautiful chaos, and it reminded me why I'd said yes to this climb in the first place. I didn't climb Kilimanjaro to escape my life. I climbed it to rediscover my strength, to step out of my comfort zone, and to prove to myself that I could do hard things.

At that moment, I felt something I hadn't felt in years: confidence. Not the fleeting kind that comes from external praise, but a deep, unshakeable belief in myself.

## The Truth About Self-Doubt

Here's what I learned on that mountain: self-doubt doesn't disappear when you accomplish something big. It's always there, whispering in the background, trying to hold you back. The key isn't to eliminate it—it's to stop letting it control you.

Self-doubt is sneaky. It shows up in the little moments: when you hesitate to share an idea in a meeting, when you don't apply for a job because you don't meet every qualification, or when you let someone dismiss your thoughts because you don't feel confident enough to speak up.

For years, I let self-doubt run the show. I told myself I wasn't smart enough, strong enough, or capable enough. And do you know what happened? I believed it.

But here's the thing: self-doubt is a liar. It tells you you're not enough when you absolutely are.

## Building Confidence, One Step at a Time

Confidence isn't something you're born with—it's something you build. It's like climbing a mountain: one step at a time, even when you're scared, even when the voice in your head is telling you to stop.

Every step I took on Kilimanjaro was an act of defiance against my doubts. Every step said, "I can do this." And by the time I reached the summit, those steps had added up to something powerful: unshakeable confidence.

## The REAL Method

Over the years, I've developed a framework for building confidence—a way to quiet the doubts and trust yourself again. I call it the REAL Method:

- **Respect your reflection:** Confidence starts with self-respect. Keep promises to yourself. Show up for yourself, even when it's hard.
- **Embrace your failures:** Failure isn't the opposite of success; it's a stepping stone. Every misstep is a lesson, not a verdict.

- **Ask yourself what you want:** Clarity is power. When you know what you want, you can take intentional steps to get there.
- **Love the woman in the mirror:** Confidence isn't about perfection—it's about acceptance. Love yourself, flaws and all.

These pillars aren't about transforming into someone else. They're about uncovering the strength that's already within you.

## What's Your Mountain?

So, what's your mountain? Maybe it's speaking up in a meeting, starting a new career, or setting boundaries in a relationship. Maybe it's saying *yes* to something that scares you or *no* to something that doesn't serve you.

Whatever it is, I want you to know this: *You are capable of more than you realize.*

Take the first step. It doesn't have to be big. It doesn't have to be perfect. Just take it. And then take another. With every step, you'll build the confidence to keep going.

The journey won't be easy. There will be doubts, setbacks, and moments when you want to quit. But when you reach the top of your mountain—whatever that looks like—you'll see what I saw: the truth that was there all along.

You are enough.

You are strong.

You are capable.

You are worthy.

Now, go climb your mountain.

# About the Curator, Leigh M. Clark

Four-time best-selling author Leigh M. Clark is known for her inspiring books, including *The Dream is in Your Hands*, *Living Kindly*, and the *Slay the USA* series. Her work as an author has empowered and motivated countless readers by highlighting kindness, resilience, and the strength of community. In addition to her writing career, Leigh has over 20 years of experience as a business strategist, working with Fortune 500 companies to help them grow and succeed.

Leigh's latest project, the Slay the USA series, is a growing national movement that shines a spotlight on extraordinary women across the country who are leaving their mark on their communities and industries. Through this series, Leigh is empowering these women to share their stories of triumph, leadership, and impact, much like she has done in her own life. The series is rapidly expanding, highlighting women in cities from coast to coast, celebrating their contributions and inspiring others to follow their lead.

Leigh's expertise and passion for leadership and empowerment have made her a sought-after speaker, with multiple appearances on the TEDx stage. Her stories of kindness and personal growth have been featured in prominent publications like *HuffPost* and shared through appearances on *The Today Show* and the *Rachael Ray Show*.

As the founder of Kindleigh, a movement focused on giving back through acts of kindness, Leigh has led initiatives that have raised significant funds for charitable causes. Her mission is to create lasting change through kindness and sharing stories of impact, further solidifying her role as a leader in philanthropy.

Leigh resides in Southwest Florida with her son, Carter, and the love of her life. She's here to make an impact and leave her mark by illuminating others.

"Don't let the world change your heart. Let your heart change the world." - Leigh M. Clark

IG:@leighmclark @slaytheusa
www.leighmclark.com
www.slaytheusa.com

www.ingramcontent.com/pod-product-compliance
Lightning Source LLC
Chambersburg PA
CBHW061758120626
46550CB00005B/2051